What Our Children Teach Us

What Our Children Teach Us

Lessons in Joy, Love, and Awareness

Piero Ferrucci

Translated by Vivien Ferrucci

WARNER BOOKS

A Time Warner Company

Warner Books, Inc., 1271 Avenue of the Americas,
New York, NY 10020
Visit our Web site at www.twbookmark.com

 A Time Warner Company

Printed in the United States of America

First Printing: April 2001
10 9 8 7 6 5 4 3 2 1

Library of Congress Cataloging-in-Publication Data
Ferrucci, Piero.
    [Bambini ci insegnano. English]
    What our children teach us / Piero Ferrucci.
        p. cm.
    ISBN 0-446-52431-X
    1. Parenthood.   2. Parent and child.   I. Title.

HQ755.8 .F4713 2001
306.874—dc21   00-044927

Contents

Introduction

Down on all fours, I am searching for a tiny plastic wheel. It has come off a toy car belonging to Emilio, my five-year-old son. He is upset. I am tired and irritated. I have already looked everywhere for this worthless object, and now I am starting all over again. Emilio really wants it. I rummage behind the divan, under the furniture, among the folds and cushions of the armchair. A reluctant slave, I move about with difficulty in these strange and dusty spaces.

Emilio tags along anxiously, following my investigation, offering advice. During my search, many thoughts crowd my brain. What am I doing, looking for this silly toy wheel? How can I stoop so low? Why do I pander to his every whim? I think about how my life has changed since my first child was born, how much of my time is spent in banal and tiresome activities like this. Sometimes I feel I am the captive of some crazed tyrant. Who was that English psychiatrist who said the family is the forge of madness? However hard I try to remember, I fail.

Then my mood changes. By some curious paradox, dealing in such small matters makes me feel bigger. As I bend low, my spirit feels higher. Simply by helping a child, I feel more open. Somehow, it does me good to remove myself from those lofty places where everything has a purpose and to waste time crawling about in a colorless world of forgotten fragments. I take myself less seriously and become a little nicer.

I even manage to find the tiny wheel—it had ended up in a crack in the floor. What a triumph! The car is once more whole, the world is functioning again. Emilio smiles.

These days my best intuitions occur during moments like this. Nothing dazzling, but when I add them all up, I have a pretty good collection. Doubtless, I used to have much more time before I became a parent. I could read, write, think. I was able to listen undisturbed to good music and to meditate, elevating my mind above my little personal sphere. I considered daily routines a distraction, if not a nuisance.

Nowadays, instead, I look for little wheels. At the end of the day, I am exhausted. Yet it seems to me that my life is far deeper and richer than it ever was before. I have come to see that each moment of parenting, no matter how annoying or trivial, has hidden surprises and opportunities for change and, at times, glimmers of wisdom.

That is the theme of this book: Living with our children enriches and transforms us. It is like doing an intensive course of study that puts us through all major life experiences, giving us a deeper understanding and a sharper attention: beauty, love, innocence, play, pain, and death, everything appears in a new light.

Another example. It is a lovely evening in late spring. The air is clear and I am walking the city streets with Jonathan, my second child, who at the time is a few months old. I hold him in my arms, feel him close to me. After observing a passing parade of cars and people, he's about to fall asleep, and he chatters to himself, his voice like some strange chant, exquisitely sweet and beautiful.

I feel I have on my chest a treasure that has been entrusted to my wife Vivien and me. A miracle, whose growth I have the daily privilege of witnessing. Right now it is his voice that fills me with wonder: a voice that says nothing, as it cannot yet form words, but says everything, because you can hear in it the pleasure and tranquillity of a baby who is at peace, who surrenders to sleep.

I hold a hand behind his head and feel the vibration of Jonathan's gurgling. These tiny vibrations have a mysterious power. They enter me and propagate in me. They transmit to me, with striking directness, his innocence. I feel immense gratitude.

This is one of the many moments when being with my children enriches me. These are moments of joy and tenderness. Afterward I am no longer the same. My anxieties and ruminations vanish. It is as if I were more in touch with life. I feel more real.

Living with our children allows us to grow. I am convinced that this is so for everyone. With children we have the opportunity to cultivate patience and humor, deepen the intelligence of the heart, learn to find hidden richness in ordinary life, find unexpected happiness.

Nevertheless, this transformation is not always painless. Alongside moments of joy there are also challenging trials, in which our weaknesses, our lies and hypocrisies, our doubts and contradictions, our shortcomings, are all brought under the most pitiless light. And yet this is how change often happens.

Here is an example. Emilio spies one of my new pens and asks, "Daddy, can I have it?" "Yes, you may . . ."

"Thank you, Dad."

". . . if you're good and don't do anything naughty."

Introduction

"Oh, well, thanks a little less," replies Emilio, skipping away, no longer interested in the pen.

Unmasked. My son mercilessly shows me, as in a mirror, my paternalistic attitude. How would I feel if someone offered me something I wanted "as long as you are a good boy"? What a disagreeable way to give! And yet that is what I am like. Emilio's reply shows me a part of myself I don't like. It may make me uncomfortable, but it changes me.

Before I had children, I would observe parents and feel a sense of superiority and self-satisfaction. Most parents seemed awkward and pathetic to me. I am a psychologist, and full of my psychological know-how, I used to note their mistakes, secretly criticize them and offer a whole lot of advice. I was sure I could do better.

Now, two children later, I am a good deal humbler. All my theories have tumbled like a house of cards. Having fallen flat on my face many times, I have lost all certitude.

But no matter. In order to understand something and move on, we have to empty ourselves of our certainty and complacency. This is the first step.

Like every parent, I have been stung, squeezed out, wounded, reprogrammed, turned inside out, never let off the hook. How often have my children, with a diabolical instinct, touched those weak points I kept carefully concealed! These episodes have transformed me.

In a hard and painful way, they have made me different from the person I was before, like no course of psychotherapy, no spiritual retreat, no meeting with an Oriental guru could have done.

Living with our children is a mine of revelations, pleasant and unpleasant. And it is a grind. Try stringing together all the meals you will have to prepare for them till they leave home. It would end in galactic outer space. The sheer slavery of it! And what about the frictions, the disappointments, the arguments, the illnesses, the bills to pay?

What parent ever anticipates any of this at the outset? I imagine all the things I could have done if I had not had children. I reminisce about the times Vivien and I could talk for five minutes without being interrupted.

And having children also brings out the darker sides of our personality. If we tend to play the victim, if we are jealous, or if we like to control others, we can really go to town with our children. If we tend to worry, we can become even more anxious: Our children are perfect subjects for the most terrifying fantasies. Our existing neuroses, rather than disappear, become amplified.

During our career as parents we may be sentenced to slavery and condemned to a life of neurosis. On the other hand, we may embark on a voyage full of insights and joys. What makes us take the better road?

Introduction

Two factors. First, the willingness to learn. We are used to thinking in terms of what we can teach our children. Maybe we need to ask ourselves what we may learn from them. After all, are they not the new arrivals, who come to us with a freshness and originality that we have perhaps lost? Aren't we the ones who go to school?

The second saving factor is the realization that the job of a parent, however mundane it may seem, has immense meaning. Look at some of the other trades: Engineers work with cement and metal; doctors with cells and organs; artists with lines and colors, sounds and images; cooks with food. Parents create life—or at least collaborate in its creation. Their prime material is human beings, whom they generate, nourish, support, and help to realize their innate potential. Could this be the highest of all arts?

This book is the fruit of one person's learning: My own experiences have been my field of study. As a psychologist used to working with inner experience, I have found it easy to note what goes on in me as I carry out the task of parenthood.

Although I am speaking only of myself, I believe that what I say applies to other parents, indeed to all who have anything to do with children. Every individual experience, although unique, contains elements belonging to all human beings.

Let us take a simple episode. Emilio is eating his cereal in silence. He is looking into the distance; it is clear that he is thinking. Not wishing to disturb his thoughts, I remain silent. Suddenly he puts down his spoon and, turning to me, asks, "Daddy, what if our whole life is just a dream?" Now, I know that children of his age are given to philosophical thought, but I am nonetheless struck by this question. "Why, yes," I answer, "one day you wake up and discover that your parents, friends, toys, and house have disappeared. You are there in bed, and you realize it was all a dream." "Yes," replies Emilio, and meanwhile resumes eating, "maybe even the bed was a dream."

It is the detail of the bed that tickles me most, because then absolutely everything is a dream, all that exists becomes ethereal and unreal. It shows me the coherence of Emilio's philosophical thinking. I am filled with awe at the mind of a child who studies the world with eyes at once innocent and intelligent.

The idea that life is a dream is one I have met in various philosophies and artistic metaphors. But as it is spoken by my own child, it takes on added vitality. I can, for a moment, see his point of view, that of a child watching the world and wondering if it is not all a creation of his own mind. And my attention, so often preoccupied with small everyday problems, suddenly grows. I rediscover the enjoyment of thinking.

Introduction

Although this episode with Emilio is unique, at the same time it is very common: Many parents are often stunned by the intelligence of their children. All parents' experiences are unrepeatable, yet it is likely that they involve some of the recurring themes. Every parent, for example, has expectations of his children. Every parent has doubts, surprises, times of boredom, and times of joy. I shall be talking about these themes. This book is a bit like a tourist guidebook—if you go to such and such a place, remember to look at that park, statue, or landscape, because it is well worth the trouble. But the journey of parenthood is much more than a tourist excursion. It can be a spiritual path, a succession of experiences that unveil the profound meaning of life.

A spiritual way takes us far. Yet the goal is near: It is what we ourselves are, our own true essence. The further we go, the more we realize that we already have everything we need. In an instant our every dissatisfaction, regret, or desire disappears. In the chaos of living, we perceive a secret perfection. We know that in the vast universe to which we belong, there is a place for us, too, and that place is where we are right now. Despite the day-to-day doubts, the fatigue, the distress, it is our own children who have taken us by the hand and led us, step by step, to that place.

What Our Children Teach Us

Attention

Emilio, three years old, has been doing lots of jumps. He must have done a hundred of them. "Daddy, Daddy, look, how do you like this jump look," he says every time. "It's a new jump!" He is very proud of his jumps.

I like the first three or four. But after a while I get bored. There, in the middle of the play park, I let my mind wander; I become inattentive.

Don't get me wrong; I love my child a lot. Even before he was born I had decided that I would spend a lot of my time with him. I was not going to be an absent father. Although we have a great relationship, after spending hour after hour with him, I have often caught myself looking at my watch, wondering when it was going to be my wife's turn to watch him.

That's when I clock off, as we jokingly say, and am free.

My little boy tugs at my sleeve: "Look, do you like this jump? Watch me!" By now there is a touch of irritation in his voice, almost a threat. "It's a new jump!" I look at my watch again. How much time is left? Two more hours, and then I can have some peace and quiet.

It has become impossible to even read the newspaper with Emilio around. He considers it an insult. At the most, I can manage to read half a column, and then: "Daaaaaaaaddy! Watch my new jump!" Now his voice is trembling with exasperation, like a schoolteacher who catches a misbehaving student.

I watch. And at last I understand: It really is a new jump. The hundredth jump is as important as the first and deserves the same attention. Emilio gives this new jump all he has got. It is a jump with a turn, followed by a kind of ballet move. For him, it is a marvelous creation. He has just finished painting *The Last Supper,* discovering the New World, formulating the Theory of Relativity. How can I possibly drift off? It is an unforgivable lapse.

Watching his hundredth jump, I once again understand the importance of attention. Often, in speaking with someone about a subject close to my heart, I see from his eyes that he is somewhere else. He is probably thinking of something more important to him. Just like

2

me and the other parents at the play park. You can almost see our thoughts coming out of our heads like comic strip balloons: money problems, sports results, weekend plans.

This absence of mind has a disintegrating effect on me. When I lose someone's attention, I speak in an emptiness, my words are merely dry leaves, scattered here and there by the wind, till finally all that is left is the sad, dead winter.

I also know the uplifting feeling I experience when I am the recipient of someone's undivided attention, without judgment and expectations. Such a feeling warms me, tells me I am important, makes me whole again. I have found this out many times in my life, yet it is easy to forget.

My child calls me back to the present moment. He can be a strict teacher who points out all my weak points and shows me the art of being in the here and now—the most important art of all. Without presence, there is no relationship, no reality.

To think about past and future is of course so much easier than living in the present. Transported away from the present, we find everything: fantasy, worries, memories. Worlds far more intriguing than watching a child jump.

In this way, removed to another time, I, like everybody else, often function on automatic pilot. I talk, drive, work, walk, eat, with just enough attention so as not to get into trouble—and sometimes not even enough for that. I return to the present only when I am brought back energetically, by pain, pleasure, or surprise.

If I am truly awake, truly in the present, everything is different. In the actual moment, none of my imagined problems has happened yet, or if any has, it appears quite different to me. The vague and menacing forms I had glimpsed in my imagination, seen in the transparency of the present, lose their power to frighten me. And the "now" no longer eludes me.

"Now" is the present. I recognize that there is nowhere else to go. Past and future exist only in my mind. I am here, now, exactly where I have always been even when I did not know it.

Suddenly the reality around me takes shape. Sounds and colors become more vivid, outlines sharper, feelings truer. Others are no longer shadows but real individuals. Each person, instead of merely belonging to a category, is this particular being. When I am aware, the world is much richer and more interesting. It is not peopled by stereotypes. Every situation is an unrepeatable event. Every jump is a new jump.

As I learn to be more aware, I notice three fundamental changes in myself. First, I see that the reality around me and in me is far richer than I thought. The less aware I am, the less interesting everything is. People, circumstances, objects, ideas are mere outlines. But when I do pay attention, they take on substance and life. The person in front of me is not simply, say, my client belonging to this or that category. He is a living being whose voice, I now notice, vibrates with timid hope. His eyes are wistful. His tie doesn't match his jacket, and his hair is combed differently from last week. He wears a strange watch on his right wrist, so he must be left-handed. Some little veins show on the tip of his nose . . . I could go on forever. This person has changed status in my perception. From being an abstraction he has become a new entity to be discovered, a new person to know. I no longer look forward to the end of the session.

Second, wherever I am, there is nowhere else to go, because I am already there. If I am living in a world of outlines, I try to get out of it as fast as I can. I do so by having a purpose and being anxious about that purpose. If I am with a friend, instead of simply enjoying his presence, I try to give a direction to our meeting: Are we getting anything done? But if I really see my friend, pay attention to his company, I have already accomplished a lot. There is a sense of healthy laziness that I have learned in being with children: Slow down, take it easy, be here, enjoy yourself. You are allowed to have no purpose.

Third, I give more of myself. I notice this one day while carrying on a conversation with Vivien, while at the same time working at the computer. I realize there is a world inside me where I retreat and entertain myself with fantasies, thoughts, and rehearsals. That's healthy. In this case, however, the computer is included in the inner world, but Vivien is not. She is merely a voice out there. That is less healthy. I am ninety percent with the computer and my thoughts, and ten percent with my wife, and the quality of our conversation is poor. I am being stingy with myself. Suddenly I decide to be present for her, as I do with my children, and it is like waking from a dream. It is gratifying to be more available. It may require an effort at first, but then I feel this is exactly where I want to be.

When I try to be present, I sometimes feel a resistance. To live in the naked present bores me; it is deceptively flat at first. Nothing seems to happen. Or else, what does happen is not what I want. I have a constant need to be stimulated and entertained.

Boredom, however, is the first sign that I am on the right track to being in the present. It means that instead of being shut up in an unreal world, I am crossing a protective barrier. The part of me that resists change tries to dissuade me from living in the present. It is a barrier that I will find sooner or later in any spiritual or intellectual adventure on which I embark and which presents me with a choice: I can go back to my unreal world. Or I can continue through the boredom of watching a hundred jumps, and then perhaps I will meet the truly new.

The art of paying attention may be practiced anywhere, at any time. It needs no guidance, techniques, or equipment. It is free and universal. Certain situations, however, facilitate it. A Zen master will sometimes move among his meditating students. With his sharp intuition he knows who is sleepy and distracted and gives the student a rap on the shoulders. Nothing aggressive, just a reminder to be aware. Children do the same thing without knowing it. Their cries, their questions and demands, are a continuous recall to the here and now, to where all is more real. Our very own place.

Very young children are always in the present. They reside there with ease and with wonder. Five-month-old Emilio watches the leaves and branches moving in the wind. His eyes move imperceptibly. He is fascinated. For him, in that moment, the branches and leaves are all there is. At two he discovers his own shadow. It follows him everywhere, and yet, what a mystery! It can disappear in a larger shadow. Or else he notices his own reflection in a puddle: Is it real, or is it a window into another world? This is being in the present. And it is a healthy contagion: I want to be like that, too.

Jonathan, at two years old, pays careful attention to

different kinds of sounds, including the faintest. He will stop suddenly and listen: an ambulance siren in the distance, the neighbor closing her window, a passerby coughing, the vacuum cleaner's whir. Then, raising a tiny finger, he looks at me and says, "That noise?" At first I didn't understand what was going on. Now I try to imagine what it is like for him, his universe full of new and indecipherable sounds.

I remember him as a newborn, lying quiet and attentive, his attention free of judgment or expectation. He fixes on nothing in particular. He is simply attentive. A state of naked awareness. I have never seen anyone pay attention like that—so completely. It is enough for me to remember those moments, and I feel better.

When we are present like they are, we can have a finer relationship with our children—indeed, with any other person. In fact, it is the only relation possible. Otherwise there are just the meetings of phantoms.

Being present means being ready and available. I am here for you. My mind does not escape into a more interesting future. It does not choose the world of fantasy, nor is it haunted by echoes of the past. With all my being, I am here for you.

I hear a clamor of protest: "But that is how you spoil a child! Nobody gives that kind of attention in the real world. The child will get used to being at center stage!"

Attention

Let me be clear: I am not referring to the kind of attention that is linked to some emotion, for example to the need to suffocate and oppress with unrequested kisses and cuddles. This is not anxious attention, always on guard lest the poor helpless child take a risk: "Watch out, you will hurt yourself!" Nor is it ambitious attention. It does not judge, nor try at all costs to find reason to correct or criticize.

It is pure attention. It does not invade or direct, but it is merely present. That is all. Such an attitude has never harmed anyone. On the contrary, it is the greatest gift we can give our children. They are used to being among so many distracted giants who, from time to time, condescend to give them a few crumbs of themselves. I am sure it means a lot to them when we place ourselves at their level, attending to what they are telling us, attending to them.

There are times when we are afraid to pay close attention. Jonathan is born, in a hospital, and I receive him in my hands: a very beautiful moment. The birth has been spontaneous, natural, and all has gone well, but the nurse has to take him from us for a few moments in order to massage him. Meanwhile, Vivien, exhausted, is helped by the midwife. In those critical instants, what do I do? I calmly go and wash my hands, distracted, outside of time, absent from the whole scene. It is a decisive moment for my loved ones, and I am out of it.

Soon enough I realize my distraction. I race to our baby and look at him, just a few moments old. He is fine, but is also kicking and protesting. I join the nurse in touching him. I speak to him, comfort him, feel a wave of love for him. I look at Vivien close by; our eyes meet. I feel for her a vast, vibrating gratitude.

What has happened? I realize it later. The emotions that surface during a birth are violent. And sometimes emotions that are too powerful frighten us. In those distracted minutes I defend myself against those very intense emotions. To see Vivien exhausted, or my baby struggling to breathe, is too much for me. So I go on and wash my hands. Then, once I recognize my fleeing, I can allow myself to feel the overwhelming anguish and the love I was trying to escape.

To pay attention is the most practical thing I can do. I see what is, and thereby I have more information. I am not taken by surprise and do not devise confused solutions to imaginary problems. Maybe a child is in a bad mood simply because he is cold, or thirsty, or his sock is slipping down into his shoe. Paying attention makes life simpler by eliminating what is superfluous. It gets to the heart of the matter.

Emilio refuses to have his hair washed. "If you let us wash your hair, we will give you a delicious snack." Emilio eats it, then refuses once again to wash his hair. "Look, there is Mummy and Daddy, and Grandmother

is coming, too, all of us in the bathroom together."
Nothing doing. "Grandma, Mummy, Daddy, another
delicious snack, and we will give you a special toy that
you can play with while we wash your hair." No way.
We might as well forget about the hair wash.

Everybody talks, yells, offers interpretations,
threats, prophesies: "If you don't wash your hair, it will
be dirty and full of little bugs!" Stories: "You know,
when Daddy was a little boy like you, he didn't want to
wash his hair, either. . . ." Empathy: "I realize you
don't like washing your hair. . . ." Sermons: "In life
there are always things we have to do; even things we
don't like." Nothing works.

Then we pay attention and try a little awareness.
How come Emilio won't let us wash his hair? Because
he is afraid water will get in his eyes. That is the real
reason. So simple. "Emilio, we will be very careful not
to let any water get in your eyes." Emilio allows us to
wash his hair. Being aware means seeing reality as it is.
It means doing away with all the browbeating and getting to the heart of all that matters.

Yes, my children have an extraordinary power to
bring me back to the present. Sometimes it almost
seems that they do it on purpose. One day I receive a
phone call, a taxation matter that drives me crazy. I
must find a receipt that I fear I may have lost, in which
case I will have to pay a fine. I am furious with myself

that my stuff is in such a mess. I feel persecuted by the tax people. As if I don't have enough to do. I will never get it all done. My inner monologue goes on in this way, a rapid gathering of black clouds.

Jonathan looks at me. He smiles. I see him as if in the distance, since I am still lost in my thoughts. I know he is there, but my worries are stronger. Why do I have to waste time in useless tasks? They will get me. I will be ruined. Jonathan keeps it up. He looks at me and smiles again. The worries begin to dissipate. Why should I spoil my life with these thoughts? I heave a sigh. Jonathan looks at me again. He is waiting, his gaze a universe in which I may enter. It is an open invitation. He smiles yet again. Now I am really with him. The black clouds have disappeared. Welcome back to the present, Dad.

Space

During our first pregnancy, Vivien and I visit the birth homes of two geniuses: Mozart and Leonardo da Vinci.

At Mozart's house in Salzburg, you can see his musical instruments and some of his manuscripts and portraits. Despite the coming and going of tourists, we somehow manage to imagine and feel his presence. In Vinci, a museum shows Leonardo's ingenious machines and mechanisms as they have been faithfully reconstructed from his drawings: the bicycle, the helicopter, the airplane, and others. You can also visit his home. It is exciting to imagine Leonardo there as a child, growing, playing, beginning to reflect and to create.

Both of these excursions enrich us and make the pregnancy even more special. For me, however, they are also symbolic. In going to Vinci and Salzburg, I hope to make contact with the miracle of genius. What if it were contagious? I confess: Deep down I want our future child to become another Leonardo or another Mozart.

No, I am not deluding myself. Genius is one in a billion. But at least my child could be gifted, capable of making an original contribution to art or science. I have always considered the human mind to be a mine of wondrous potentialities. To raise a child means to see this reality at work.

There is no harm in this way of thinking. In fact, if each of us were to acknowledge the exceptional element in ourselves, the world would only get better. But in my attitude toward my unborn child, there is an almost compulsive ambition. Fear, too. What if I have a mediocre child? How awful! No, my child has to be special, and I will do everything I can to help him be so. I have read all the scientific research on how to encourage all of my child's talents. I can't wait to see the realization of his gifts.

Only after some time do I realize how these expectations make me pedantic and heavy. And I see that Emilio's true development has nothing to do with my fantasies. He has his own pace, his own independent drive, his own destiny.

I learn this lesson when Emilio is a couple of months

old. I have read lots of books on how to turn your child into a genius, and I start making him do gymnastics for newborns. This training stimulates connections between brain cells, the books assure us. But despite their promises of a joyous response from the baby, I notice that Emilio often turns his head away when I try to train him—the sign of aversion in a baby. He does not cry—I handle him very gently—but neither is he enthusiastic.

It takes very little for me to understand: Emilio does not want to perform these exercises. They are an intrusion, and he has no way of defending himself. I step back, just look, and enjoy his spontaneous movements in all their beauty. Like all babies, he knows very well how to do gymnastics in a way far more complete and organic than I can ever teach him. I see that Emilio is fine as he is, without need of correction. His movements make a naturally aesthetic performance, like the dance of dolphins or the sprint of a cheetah.

At first this intuition is painful. Emilio will not be a genius after all. Or at least I won't be able to make him exceptionally intelligent. It is the death of a dream. But then I feel relief. I give him permission, inside me, to be what he is. Perhaps he will be an ordinary child. I realize that I no longer have control of the process. I shrink to size as well: No more a Pygmalion, I become a mere assistant. But straight afterward I see him as he is, perfect without interference. This is the state of grace—instead of anxiety and compulsion, I enjoy the simple pleasure of being.

Dreams of greatness, I realize, are a family tradition. My mother wanted me to be a superachiever. From the beginning she tried in various ways to stimulate my intelligence. I still remember how proud she was in telling the "train story." I was two years old, sitting on a train, and I started reading the newspaper of the person in front of me out loud. The passengers in the compartment were amazed.

All my mother's expectations have weighed on me—however much she loved me. Even now, after so many years, I sometimes have the feeling I am living an existence that is not entirely mine, a life whose course has been decided by someone else. If I have an ambition, for example, I am not sure it is really mine. Maybe I am trying to satisfy my mother's desires, or the need of someone who is no longer here, but whose expectations live on in me. And I risk doing the same to Emilio.

Understanding this lesson is a long way away from assimilating it, however. In the school of life I am a slow student, and I have to tackle the same lesson many times. Four months later, Jonathan is nine months old and is learning how to eat. According to the growth charts, he is a little underweight. According to the visible evidence, he is in splendid health, cheerful and full of vitality. But as a genuinely anxious parent, I believe more in the growth chart than in my own eyes. When Jonathan eats, I think mainly about how much he is eating. Is it enough? How much protein is he absorbing? Will this food help him grow?

Fortunately, Jonathan is in another framework altogether. For him, eating is a party. He does not want to be strapped in his high chair—who would?—but prefers to stand up and sway. He blows raspberries, watches his brother playing, flirts with a visiting friend, offers me food, throws around bits of prune or spoonfuls of vegetable soup, tells his stories, takes a slice of banana in his fist, squeezes it, dumps it on my head, laughs, yells out for water to drink, performs balancing acts with the spoon, and if ever he actually introduces food into his mouth, the sensation of taste is so intense that his whole body responds with a kind of dance that almost makes him fall off the high chair.

I nevertheless sit there in front of him, without participating in the party. I worry. Is he eating or isn't he? I only want him to keep up with the growth charts.

Then one day I have an insight. For a moment when I am not expecting anything, a crack opens and I understand. I see this performance. I see that Jonathan does not divide the world into categories. For him, there is no such thing as just eating. A meal is also a time for dancing, relating to people, enjoying, speaking, studying the laws of gravity, exploring all his senses, playing, everything at once. In this world there are no divisions. It is whole. I begin to enjoy this meal and look forward to the next show.

What have I learned? As long as I expect my children to be a certain way, I am tense and worried, cannot see them as they are, and cannot have any pleasure from being with them. I am a policeman. But when I give up my expectations, I am more in touch with my children and enjoy myself and them much more.

I notice myself becoming more sensitive to others' behavior toward me in this respect. Some people expect me to be a certain way, or judge me because I am not. Others let me be who I am—these relationships are invariably better. How refreshing it is to be with somebody who does not put me in a straitjacket! I want to be that way, too. I realize that I can relate to others either with expectations or with support and appreciation. It is a fundamental difference, and I am slowly becoming better able to choose between the two.

I also realize that when I have high expectations of others and myself, I become tense and stern. There is an element of fear, too—fear of being let down. When I have fewer or no expectations, I am much more relaxed, because I realize we all make mistakes, we are all grossly imperfect, and we seldom reach our goals precisely as planned. This is the virtue of humility. Judgments and expectations are cold and serious, humility is warm and funny, because it helps us understand how pathetic we all can be, and accept it, and smile about it. Trouble is just around the corner: A clerk miscounts my change and keeps me waiting, my collaborators at the training center make a mistake, or I cannot find the car keys—again. The armies of judgment arise, ready to fire. But I send them back to the barracks. It's okay to be clumsy. It's okay to be human.

There is no one on earth, I am sure, who has not felt the burden of someone else's expectations. "I want you to be like this," expressed more or less explicitly, is the formula permeating relations between people. Sometimes it is absent at the beginning of a friendship or a romance, in those magical times when two people are simply enjoying and getting to know each other. Later, the duties, rules, demands, expectations, guilt feelings sneak in, and the freshness of those early moments vanishes.

Living with the weight of expectations is tiring for anyone, especially for a child: Her personality is being formed and she is more vulnerable than an adult. Yet not a single child is free of this burden. I see it happening all the time. At Emilio's first birthday we attend a reunion of the prenatal group. All the children are his age. They can all walk—except for one. His father is annoyed with him. "Wake up!" he tells him, as he pulls him up by the hands and tries to make him walk. The baby would like to stay sitting and look around. He has not the slightest desire to walk. But his dad wants him to keep up with the others.

Expectations. You can see them everywhere: "Be a real boy!," and the child becomes a little macho with a gun and a motorbike. "Be a true girl!," and the young girl becomes a little temptress with painted fingernails. Thus children are turned into pretty knickknacks, supergifted monsters, sports champions, or just good little puppets who never get into trouble because they are already only half alive.

Expectations are like those tiny shoes Chinese women had to wear so their feet would be small and they would delight men with their wobbly step. They succeed in having you accepted, but at what price? An expectation prevents a child from developing according to his own inner laws and instead imposes an arbitrary norm from the outside.

It is as if I were to infiltrate my children's very core, set up my headquarters there, and live my own life through them, depriving them of all power. How does it feel to have an army occupy your being? A child under the weight of excessive or inappropriate demands must deny or mask her own impulses and interests, values and thoughts. She thinks they are not good enough. She wants to please and strives to meet the demands. She does not trust her own judgment and does not even know who she is.

When I urge my child to be the way I want him to be, I stop him from being who he is. But I also prevent myself from being who I am, because I no longer live in myself. I live in my child and have lost myself. Expecting him to be a certain way takes effort. Installing myself in him in order to direct his life causes me to emigrate from myself. I am alienated from my own life, and I am vulnerable. I bet all my chips on events outside my control—a game I am bound to lose.

One day I go to the park with Emilio. I expect him to run around, explore the equipment, exercise all his muscles, make friends with other children. But he has something else in mind. He stands by himself in one corner and pretends he is a train. This game consists in his running a hand along one of the parallel bars. His hand is the train, stopping at each station. I am supposed to put two fingers on his hand—that is me getting on the train. I am the only one who can get on and off, and this game cannot be played anywhere else.

The other children play on swings, slides, they throw balls and climb up ladders, go on the merry-go-rounds, and run happily everywhere. But not he. He has to be a train, back and forth, from one imaginary station to another, for one hour. And I have to follow him with my two fingers on his hand—woe betide me if I lose a moment's attention.

Every now and again the other children and their parents look at us as if to say, What on earth are those two doing? I respond with embarrassed little smiles, as if to say, Well, he is only a child. I muse that this is a game we can do at home on a rainy day, that Emilio is missing an opportunity to move his body, grow strong, socialize. I want to say, Why don't you play like all the other children? Why aren't you like them?

But I restrain myself, recognizing that I would prevent him from enjoying himself in his own way, from being himself. When we went to the science museum, all he wanted to do was ride up and down in the elevator. Emilio's refusal to do what he was supposed to do, and what everyone else was doing, made me uncomfortable. And yet, creativity consists of following your original impulses. That is why creative people are seen as strange and are often ridiculed. Children are capable of expressing their originality as long as we adults do not force them to think like we do—a constraint we then welcome with relief and call "maturation."

So I play the train with Emilio. Who cares if other people think we are strange? I am used to it by now. I play his way. No more reservations. I trust him because I sense that his physical and mental development are governed by an intelligence best left alone, without in-

terference from me or anyone. I no longer try to ma-
nipulate him into playing a certain way. Now I understand why he needs to play like this and not in any
other way. I rediscover the pleasure of play.

If I try to impose my expectations, I end up transforming pleasure into obsession. Some parents make an
art of it. I have met children for whom playing the violin is a torture, soccer a nightmare, dancing forced
labor. Friends, music, books, sports, art, theater, all can
become horrible monsters that we, with our best intentions, teach our children to abhor for the rest of their
lives.

A big insight along the same lines comes to me when
we move to the country. This is a huge change in our
lifestyle. We decide to get away from the car fumes of
the city because we want our child to grow up in nature, sunlight, fresh air. We find the right house. Now
we are going to realize our nature-loving ideal.

Soon enough, however, we discover, to our dismay,
that Emilio is not in the least interested in fresh air:
"Don't like outside." This child looks pale to us, and he
surely needs at least two hours a day outdoors to run
and jump in the sun. So we try a few tricks to lure him
out. But with uncanny skill, Emilio always senses our
hidden intentions and never falls in the trap. Nature
and fresh air become an obsession.

Luckily, Vivien and I become aware of our mistake

and stop. Now Emilio collects leaves and berries, runs and jumps outdoors, observes the ripening of fruits, makes friends with the animals, follows the phases of the moon and the variations of the weather, but only if and when he wants to, for his own interest and liking—not for being the way we want him.

Why do I feel such a compelling desire to realize my expectations through my children? Now I know. I try to realize, through them, all that I have not achieved myself.

In the course of my life, while interested in many subjects, I have specialized in philosophy and psychology. Up to now I have had a full and interesting time, yet I am by no means satisfied. Sometimes the world of the psyche seems vague and unclear, and my work too subjective. I think about how interesting it would have been to delve into science—biology, for instance, or astronomy. They are so precise, so reassuringly clear. At other times I think how wonderful it would have been to explore the world of art. I feel incomplete.

This sense of incompleteness is, after all, a part of life itself and can never be overcome, except perhaps in rare moments. But that thought does not console me, and the dissatisfaction remains. The natural outlet is to direct my children to those interests, because I know they are beautiful and worthwhile.

This means I am trying to realize myself through

them. It may seem awful, yet it is so: I use my children to satisfy my own aspirations. Think about it a moment, and you will agree that this task is both unfair and impossible. It is a kind of psychic parasitism that harms all involved. I am horrified at the thought. My children must live their lives, not mine. Of course, I will expose my kids to art and science, but freely, as a possibility, not as a fixed rail on which to travel. And certainly not in order to relieve me of my frustration, my mistakes, my dissatisfaction.

I return to myself, alone with my incompleteness. Dealing with my children shows me my own difficulties. I am aware of my limits, mistakes, insecurities. Maybe I even think that I have failed—that I have thrown my life away.

But then I realize that it is the mistakes and the dissatisfaction that help me learn, try again, and improve. In a happy moment I glimpse the possibility of accepting myself as I am—incomplete, responsible for my mistakes, at times banal. It all seems to be woven into a huge tapestry in which I can begin to perceive some sense. I feel a vast serenity pervading my life and the lives of others. Anxiety vanishes.

I see my children in a different way, and I feel able to see life from their point of view. Jonathan looks at a pebble, fascinated, rolling it around several times in his hands. Emilio remains speechless with wonder when he sees and hears a chamber orchestra for the first time in his life. I watch them with pleasure and tenderness. I expect nothing of them, neither judge them nor compare them to other children. I accept them as they are. I feel free.

Bit by bit I also discover new ways of loving. After all, how can I truly love my children if at the same time I wish they were different? Emilio pesters his brother. He pinches his cheek, pushes him, pokes him. Jonathan usually takes it all in stride, even laughs. Sometimes, however, he cries. It is a situation to be handled with tact. I do not want to humiliate Emilio, jealous of his new little brother, who arrived only a few months ago. I tell him, "Dear Emilio, I love you very much, but you must stop tormenting Jonathan." Emilio looks at me, smiles, then says, "I knew you would say 'but.'"

What a lesson. So, I love him, but . . . I place myself in Emilio's shoes. How hard it must have been for him to adapt to this little brother whom everybody loves and raves about. How hard it must have been not to be the center of attention anymore. Discipline is important, but it can wait. I postpone it. I find out what it means to say "I love you" in an unconditional way. What a relief. My old way of loving now appears to me as tedious bargaining: I offer you A in exchange for B. I love you if you do B. Now, instead, I love, and there is not a single cell in my body that says "no," "if," "but." I feel whole. I say to Emilio, "Dear Emilio, from now on I will love you with no buts." "I love you with no buts" comes to be a saying in our family. It does not mean that Emilio is allowed to give Jonathan a hard time. But strangely enough, ever since I started loving him without buts, he has stopped.

If I had to sum up all these discoveries in one word, I would say "space." All too often we take other people's space away from them. We tell them how they should be, what they should do, we make up plans for them, dictate conditions, judge and blackmail. How much more gracious to surround another, especially a child, with space—to let him breathe, and give only the support he really needs. When we offer freedom, we feel freer. If we give space, we feel more spacious, too.

The Past

We are at the beach. A three-year-old girl tries to make friends with Emilio. He is a little embarrassed but likes the idea. At a loss for what to do, Emilio sits down with a thump in the sand. The little girl responds with a smile and straightaway does the same. Next, Emilio, a bit more at ease, stands up and then thumps down again in the sand. The girl does the same once again, as if to say, Look, I am just like you, we can be friends. By now Emilio is also smiling. So they go on: another thump by the girl, another by Emilio. They are in synchrony. But in the middle of the ritual, the little girl's mother arrives on the scene and says, "Come on, we have to go." The little girl leaves with her mother, casting one last sad look at Emilio.

What made the woman interrupt such a beautiful

rite of friendship? Half an hour later, I see her and her daughter still on the beach: She did not really have to go away at all. Perhaps she did not like her daughter making friends in such an original way. Perhaps it was because good girls are not supposed to talk with strangers. Maybe she was uncomfortable with Emilio's nakedness, whereas her daughter was wearing a pretty, lacy, feminine swimsuit. Whatever the case, in that moment she transmitted her standoffishness to her daughter, who may, in turn, perpetuate it in her own future life. What a pity.

Yet such an event is by no means rare; in fact, it is the very fabric of life with our children. In a TV ad for a famous chocolate spread, in an atmosphere of perfect serenity, a mother says to her daughter, "When I was little, my mummy used to spread this chocolate on my bread, just as I am doing for you now." The same thing happens with our neuroses. We adults spread our neuroses, attitudes, habits, prejudices, mannerisms, and complexes on the daily bread of our kids. Thus our children become a kind of reincarnation of ourselves, as we are of our parents. How much of our father and mother lives in us? Probably a lot—however rebellious and original we may think we are. Seen in this way, the family is a kind of business whose chief goal is to perpetuate itself through the generations.

Let us start at an elementary level. I once had an

uncle who was very funny and popular with us children. He liked to do magic tricks and play practical jokes, like offering plastic cakes or wearing a little gadget that gave a tiny electric shock when you shook his hand. However, he also had a very annoying habit. He would point his finger and spiral it toward us, poking it hard at our abdomen, while making a loud hissing sound like a balloon deflating.

This act irritated me a lot. I hated the way that finger poked my belly, the way it invaded my physical space. But I would not say a word for fear of offending my uncle. It was one of those little indignities—like tickling or teasing—to which all children are subjected, which if aimed at an adult would be considered extremely disrespectful. To my own surprise, I soon enough found myself playing the same joke on Emilio, who would retreat after I poked him, smiling sheepishly. When I realized what I was doing, I asked him if he liked it, and he replied no. Even still, as though moved by an automatic motor, I repeated the joke several times before stopping altogether.

Thus, even the least significant act comes back up to the surface many years later. We are dealing not only with mannerisms or silly pranks, however, but also with mental habits and attitudes, even entire lifestyles. Looking through my notes, I find the "supermarket example." Emilio suddenly decides he has had enough of following me around with the grocery cart and starts running down the aisles, laughing. This game of "now you see me, now you don't" is great fun. *"Un bel gioco dura poco,"* I tell Emilio after playing the game for a while. "All good things must come to an end." Just like the lady at the beach, I tell him that it is time to go. But for a child all good things should go on and on. With a wicked smile he challenges, "Daddy, let's lose each other!"

"And what if we really do?"

"Never mind," he replies, and runs away.

I go along with it, but one by one the anxieties from the past rush into my brain: People in the supermarket will get upset, this place is enormous and you can really get lost, we are attracting everyone's attention, why don't I make Emilio obey me for once? All my old conditioning shows its strength. But I do not give in to these voices from the past and continue playing. Instead of taking Emilio into my world, I let him take me into his. I have everything to gain. And in fact, at the end, despite one or two dirty looks from other customers, I feel happy and free. That is because I have shaken off the inhibitions of the past. Deep inside, I was still a child who had been told to be a good boy and not to run in stores. Of course, it is commendable to follow the rules, but maybe I was just a bit too uptight. In this case, the free child—Emilio—freed the imprisoned one—me.

Another example. I am rock climbing with Emilio. While I trudge cautiously over the rocks, he leaps, flexible and light of step. I can already imagine him fallen, cut, and bruised, but I say nothing because I cannot stand those other parents who continually warn their children, "Watch out!," "Don't touch that!," "Come back!" That is the surest technique for creating fearful, uptight kids. A cry of anguish that echoes across the generations.

Although this fear is hard to drop, I manage to control myself for a while. But when Emilio reaches the most dangerous rock, all my accumulated anxiety explodes in the cry, "Stop! Watch out!" I can still see the scene replayed in slow motion. In Emilio's body, which till then had been working so well, there is a short circuit: It becomes tense, he loses his balance, falls, and cries—not only for hurting himself, I believe, but because I have conveyed to him my own fear.

Obviously, if Emilio had really been at risk, I would have warned him. But he was not. Still, I was anxious, in the same way the grown-ups around me had been with me when I was a child. I was in the prison of anxiety. This time I extended it to Emilio.

We transmit to our children a whole host of feelings and behaviors at all levels: a fear of spiders, sexual shame, attitudes toward food, property, and money, fear of death. It usually happens without explanations.

There is no explicit consent, rather a kind of osmosis. A character trait or a habit is not delivered to us in a package. It reaches us by contagion.

How much of our individuality actually survives? After all, our personal growth is the expression of all that differentiates us from others, our distinctive style and unique contribution. Our individuality. But often we fail to grow and our individuality is submerged in a personality that is not ours. Thus we repeat habits transmitted from one generation to the next.

In the here and now, the past acts as the Great Thief, repeating itself in the form of mental and emotional habits, robbing the present of its uniqueness and freshness. In a universe that is new at every moment, we end up producing only imitation, because to repeat is easier than to invent. We feel safer, more accepted by others.

Having a child impresses this fact most forcefully upon us. In time, we all have learned to coexist with our big and small neuroses. Even if they accompany us all our lives, we take them for granted and often almost forget them. Other people see them in us, we do not. But the moment we pass them on to another person who is innocent and vulnerable, then they become visible and tangible to us, too. They manifest themselves to us with embarrassing exactitude.

For example, one day I am with Emilio in a play park. When other children come up to us with an attitude ever so slightly hostile, I feel a strange disquiet. I realize it is the echo of an old panic and suddenly recall a forgotten episode from my childhood: a bucket of sand tipped onto my head, the feeling of being attacked, the crude, primitive world of power struggles that you find among children. This is my past. Yet somehow I manage to transmit it to Emilio without saying a word. Perhaps it is with an imperceptible gesture, or a subtle, empathic resonance in our common unconscious. He cannot do much about this. But I can. My past comes back to me. I can either relive the fear or conquer it, redeem it, and therefore change myself. I stop interfering with Emilio's reaction and retreat. Emilio can deal with those children; maybe they are not hostile after all. And indeed, so it happens.

This is a common experience: While living with our children we relive our own childhood. Often that is beautiful and wholesome. Jonathan is eating his pappa verde, and I remember when I as a child ate that same green vegetable on the gray marble table of our kitchen. It all comes back to me, the taste of the soup, the golden spoonful of olive oil added to it, the warm glow of that time. As Emilio designs a rocket, I flash back on the rocket I once planned with my friends and recall the excitement, the adventure, the happiness. I believe this is one of the great nourishing factors of bringing up a child. As our children grow, we revisit our own past and tread again the path we once trod. We feel our roots again and understand how we have become what we are.

Our past, however, is not filled only with wholesome memories. It is also full of big and small traumas, frustrations, misadventures, disillusionments. All these events are not just stored as computer files. Instead, they live on and color our present life. In the play park, I relived a past incident. At that moment I had a choice: Let the past repeat itself in the form of a shy and restrained attitude and risk transmitting that fear to my son, or be in the present. I chose to be here and now. Children call us back to the present by showing how much we still live in the past. The past is our chain. Children help us to break that chain.

The traits that surface on these occasions are not always those transmitted by our parents. They may be our own childish traits that we have never confronted and that have taken hold of our lives without our being fully aware of what was going on. Now our children hold them up for us to see.

I am at the grocery shop with Emilio. The shopkeeper, concentrated and serious, is slicing ham. Emilio, whom I have picked up in my arms, points to him and says, "What is his name?" I reply, "Ask him." Emilio asks him, but in a faint voice, perhaps because of the shyness he feels at that moment in me. The shopkeeper carries on. He looks even more serious. You are not supposed to ask personal and irrelevant questions of someone engaged in work. We must not disturb him. Then I realize that right now I am a scared child in a world of distant and threatening adults. That shyness that I had felt as a child had become a constant companion that I had taken for granted. Suddenly it is no longer so. It is a very solid and evident block with which I must come to terms. But for Emilio it is different. He is facing the world, learning how to form relationships. What am I to do? If I say we must not disturb the man, I affirm my shyness and communicate it to him. Instead, with some effort and feeling like a fool, I ask him, "Excuse me, what is your name?" He looks at us, a little perplexed, then smiles, tells us his name, makes a few jokes. The whole scene changes. I have shown my son that other people are not bogeymen. And how could I have done this, had I not seen it myself?

This episode changes me. Not that I go around asking people's names in shops. But I feel more comfortable with myself when I am with others. I take a new look at my interactions with them. As I loosen up, I understand better the meaning of our social conventions and see them for what they are: useful habits we acquire as children—not terrifying imperatives.

Jonathan has taken me a step further. Like many

toddlers, he has an extraordinary capacity for relating to others. It is a gift that, as adults, we often partly lose. I had forgotten about it. In my contacts with people there is usually a utilitarian element: We are here to do. Having some preestablished purpose is a powerful defense from others. I had almost forgotten how nourishing and entertaining a relationship could be for its own sake.

Jonathan, eighteen months, knows nothing of this. He goes around in public places, buses, elevators, railway stations, lines at the post office, and starts to observe people, looking at them with such intensity that they simply cannot ignore him. Some light up; you see that they are flattered. Others are embarrassed, perhaps even frightened. But he does not give up. He is capable of staring at them for a long time. He smiles at them, waves, plays "now you see me, now you don't" with his head. In the end, even the stiffest surrender and relax.

There is absolutely nothing utilitarian in this game. It is as if he were saying, Here we are. How nice! I can see he enjoys the pure fact of relating, of being with me this moment. He studies me, as though asking, What's this? I tell him, This is Dad. He smiles. How wonderful to be able to wave all my worries good-bye, and simply to be with Jonathan!

We are on the train and Jonathan is walking up and

down, exploring. Finally he starts staring at a gentleman who is half asleep. Jonathan stands in front of
him, looks at him, and points. The poor guy is a little
uneasy. I plunge into panic. Jonathan is transgressing
all my oldest social inhibitions. I do not even know
where they come from, but here they are: You just do
not invade other people's space. You just cannot be that
forward. Better to keep a veil between us all, which
dulls the emotions, hides and protects us. But no. The
gentleman, after a moment or two of tension, smiles.
Suddenly I remember what I have always known: It is
a pleasure to be with people; we can enjoy each other.

Yes, the world of children is too urgent to leave
room for that which is spurious or outdated in me. I will
not say I have eliminated all of my own unnecessary
childhood notions, but my children make me see them
in all their absurdity and incipience. The past, which
previously lived in me like a silent parasite without my
knowing it, now seems useless and dried up. It is a fos-
sil and, like other fossils, is best left in a museum.

Identity

I play with Emilio before going to work. At some point he sticks on my forehead a picture of a clown playing a trumpet. He is amused and we both laugh. After a while, I say good-bye and go to work. But I forget about the sticker. My psychotherapy clients don't tell me anything. I see that they have a funny expression today, all of them. For some mysterious reason, my sessions are better than usual; they are happy and uninhibited. Only in the evening, while driving home, do I realize that the sticker is still pasted to my forehead. I would describe it in this way: Emilio has disintegrated my professional role.

Who am I? I am a psychologist, I am a husband, I am a father. That is my conventional identity. That is how I introduce myself to others. It is a kind of shorthand that I, like all of us, use in everyday life to escape chaos. Roles are practical: I cannot sit down and tell the story of my life on every occasion. Roles simplify. I go to a doctor, for instance, knowing she will not behave like a traveling salesman. It is reassuring: If I have a role, I am somebody. That's what makes everyday life work.

There is, however, a problem: We grow attached to our roles, and we end up mistaking them for our true identity. Our false and incomplete self takes over. We become the facade, while the mysterious and creative soul is lost.

Roles are predictable, stereotyped. They are not who we are. We are much more original and interesting than our roles suggest. If we want to grow, we have to give up the reassuring protection of roles. The facade has to crack open. And through the crack we will be able to glimpse a richer and more vital world.

This is where children come in. Why? Because they have an extraordinary talent for breaking apart our roles. Watching my roles fall apart has been an intense experience, at times painful, at others funny. There is a phase, for example, in which Emilio becomes furious every time I answer the telephone. I can understand his frustration: I come home in the evening, he hasn't seen me during the day, and he wants my company without interruptions. I read him a story and the phone rings—

one, two, three, four times. It is not fair, but I have to answer; it is part of my work. So he takes his revenge. He starts screaming, or pressing the buttons on the phone, and makes any conversation ridiculous or impossible.

What goes on at the other end of the line? These may be my clients or, worse still, potential clients, who, with uncertainty and trepidation, are calling me for the first time. What do they think when they hear the pandemonium—my scuffle with Emilio as he tries to reach the buttons, his furious shrieks, the telephone crashing to the ground? One time, while I was trying to keep him away from the telephone, he, with artful malice, shouted several times, "You are hurting me, you are hurting me!" The potential client with whom I was speaking said good-bye in a hurry and never turned up again.

My entire professional identity is at stake when he docs this. In such moments, I feel stripped naked. My role as competent psychologist with a balanced and harmonious life starts to flounder, just as it does when I am working and suddenly notice my son's dribble marks on my clothes. All at once I become more human and more vulnerable. I realize my clients perceive me quite differently.

My self-disclosure happens to be useful in the work I do. The relevant point here, however, is that my professional mask is crumbling, and with it all the security it may have offered me. Now I have fewer defenses. And I, too, see myself differently.

Exactly the same principle is at work in another of my roles, one I am particularly attached to: The Writer. For years as a free bachelor, whenever time allowed, I would write books—only a few, but thoroughly researched and cared for. I used to set aside entire empty days for writing. It was a kind of ritual. I used only white paper, perfectly sharpened pencils, and the computer. My glass desk near the window had to be empty and perfectly clean. It had to mirror the sky.

I would then open to the inspiration of the Muse. I wrote, and felt important. I felt I had something to say to the world.

Now the scene is different. Toy construction pieces, leftover biscuits, Emilio's drawings, the babysitter's hair clip, last week's unread newspaper, Jonathan's knickknacks, letters I have not had time to answer, shopping lists, pebbles and berries, drinking straws, the horribly smudged computer screen . . . this is the landscape on my desk. Forget about the sky.

These days, the only time left for me to write without being disturbed is the early morning. I can count on it only until an imperious cry from the bedroom reaches my ear. The day begins. The Father enters. The Great Writer vanishes.

And what of the gender role? According to some research, being a parent accentuates one's sexual identity: A man becomes more of a man, a woman more of a woman. Not so for me. I have become more of a woman. In fact, I have realized that, apart from several physiological functions, such as giving birth and breast-feeding, we are all pretty much the same. Fathers and mothers alike are all capable, if we choose, of loving our kids, protecting, nurturing, stimulating, and guiding them, of playing with dolls or with toy trains. Being a parent has allowed me to overcome the artificial barriers between the two genders. It has helped put me in touch with acts and sentiments traditionally assigned to women—nurturing, tenderness, protectiveness—from which men in our society are generally exiled.

I notice this change at the play park one day, when I talk with a few mothers about the best brand of diapers. Suddenly a wave of anxiety hits me, and I feel a compelling desire to run away and deal in exclusively male matters—whatever that may be.

But I wait. Anxiety is the bread and butter of my profession. I observe it and face it squarely, because I know it may conceal a surprise. Indeed, I uncover, inside myself, a hidden world I did not know, another part of me capable of caring for others in small everyday matters, walking slowly, watching a little tree grow day by day, and generally being in contact with life in its less spectacular and intense aspects, warmth and care and gentleness without ulterior purpose. Call it the feminine side if you wish. I prefer not to name it, simply to regard it as another part of myself.

Discoveries galore. One day I have a kidney stone—a brief but terribly painful affliction. In my case it turns out to be much less serious than it feels. The ambulance takes me to the emergency unit. Even though I am in pain, I feel impatient and cannot wait to get out, regard the kidney stone much as I would a common cold, and in a few hours I am rid of it and back at home that very evening. Not so ten years before, when, in the same condition, frightened, I suspended all activities for two weeks and had a stream of visitors coming to reassure me I was not dying.

Now I have no time to worry about myself. I am at the front line, taking care of others, and cannot afford to be ill. I am no longer overwhelmed by small misfortunes. I feel more resilient. This is a side of myself I had lost touch with, and I am happy I have met it again.

All discoveries are useful, though they may not be equally encouraging. One day, for example, I find out that I am not as libertarian as I once thought. I have always believed myself to be democratic in raising my children. Many people criticize me for being too permissive. The idea of placing limits on children—as everybody tirelessly preaches—has always been uncomfortable for me. It seems a worn-out, unacceptable cliché. I like it that my children are anarchic and willful. I am glad if they have the space to express what they want. It seems to me that obedience and conformity have been the cornerstone for the worst crimes committed by humanity.

A surprise awaits me. What I think I am and what I really am are two different matters. At one point I am having a lot of conflict with Emilio. He never does what I tell him. "Wash your ears!" "No!" "It's time to get dressed." "No way." "Let's go, we are late." "You go!" "Come to dinner"—it is as if I had not spoken. The democratic, broad-minded personality starts to flounder, and irritation sets in. On many of these occasions I find myself saying, "You have to do as I say, and that's that." If Emilio does not obey immediately, I feel offended. Astonishment wells up in me at this shocking effrontery: How dare he?

When all is well, I am an anarchist and a libertarian, but when things get out of hand, I opt for the line of least resistance: dictatorship. I am usually easygoing with Emilio, then suddenly, when in a hurry, tired, or irritated, I shift to the older and more deeply rooted method of parenting—the authority that decides without explaining and affirms itself without allowing compromise: Do as you are told.

Yes, we all tell ourselves nice stories about ourselves, but they may not coincide at all with the reality of who we are. The light, visible side of the moon serenely shines. But let's not forget the dark side. To be complete, we have to know both.

Take anger, for example. I have never felt an anger as vehement as that which I have felt toward Emilio. It is a rage whose intensity astonishes me. I normally consider myself to be a fairly reasonable person. Yet with Emilio, my own son whom I love so very much, I sometimes feel a volcanic anger welling up in me. Jonathan is too young to enrage me, but perfectly capable of driving me crazy, such as when he wakes up every twenty minutes and turns from a calm little baby into a disconcerting enigma.

The same applies to other feelings, like depression and despair. At times I feel robbed of my freedom, invaded, imprisoned in a life that is no longer my own. I feel I have lost myself, captive of the life I have helped create, slave to a thankless, senseless labor that has no end. I believe I have failed in bringing up my children, and, as in a nightmare, I see myself in the future: My sons become delinquent, or they abandon me in my old age. I cultivate fantasies of dying, or of disappearing without a trace. These are the abysses.

Luckily, I do not act out the anger, nor do I really believe in the despair. Yet these emotions exist, new, intense, at times horrifying. My children put me in touch with parts of myself I never knew about. I know that I must get acquainted with these horrid and violent sides of myself, in order to be closer to wholeness.

While I have at times reached full intensity of anger or unhappiness, it is also true that with my kids I have attained heights of love and joy so great that a few moments are worth years of doubt and disappointment. I am putting Jonathan to sleep and, as we often do, we are listening to an adagio by Mozart. I hold him close and rock him. His total surrender is one of life's extraordinary gifts. I am filled with gratitude. Or, looking at Emilio, his golden curls, his cheeky smile, his delicate features, I am struck by his beauty. Sometimes all it takes is a laugh from Emilio or Jonathan, a word, a gesture, seeing them asleep, or half an hour's play together, for me to think, Now I have reached a state of happiness so complete that I could die at this moment.

I sense that I am expanding in yet another dimension: not only in the depths and the heights of the psyche, but also in time. Before having children, I felt like an entity disconnected from history. Only now am I aware that I am playing in the game of generations, the sequence that has been going on for hundreds and thousands of years in the human family: We are born, we grow, we reproduce, we grow old, we die, and our children start the cycle over again. An ever-turning wheel.

I realize it one day with a shock. Emilio, annoyed because I refuse to let him use my camera, says that when I die he will take possession of everything I own. Here, suddenly, I face the brave new generation. When I was still unmarried and without children, I was just an overgrown kid. No one stood in my way. No one threatened to take over, to take my place in society—and play, create, enjoy life while I turn to dust. I am anguished.

But soon enough I am serene again: I see my part in a chain of existence far bigger than me. I feel connected to those who came before me, the generation of my parents, which I know well, that of my grandparents, a fainter memory, of the great-grandparents my parents sometimes talked about, and of the ancestors in the distant past. I think that perhaps I, too, will be a grandfather, and imagine the kind of relationship I shall have with my grandchildren. I wonder about the different world in which they will live, perhaps devastated by ecological catastrophes, or perhaps more open and harmonious. I think about what it will be like, in turn, for their children, for whom I will be but a remote entity.

Some aspect of myself will live on in my descendants, even though they will not know it—a way of thinking, or a trait, a habit—just as I, unknowingly, embody some aspect of my own ancestors. I imagine distant generations, past and future, with whom I, too, share some trait, and I view our human existence with a more detached eye. I see our life as but an instant in a vast time span, a time that reframes any claim to importance. No longer am I an isolated individual in a spurious present. Rather, I am part of a huge undertaking carried on through the centuries. I feel I am a participant in the human family.

My identity now seems to have extended and taken new forms. It is richer, more varied. As my awareness grows, I acquire a far broader view of my self. I have changed.

You Are That

I am tired and irritated. We should not have come to town with the children. Vivien is in a similar state, regretting the whole trip. It was a messy and enervating affair. The children are hungry, and we decide to have a snack in a self-service restaurant for tourists—the sort of place I have always tried to avoid. The children can feel our agitation. I am giving Jonathan some pieces out of an enormous cup of fruit salad. Emilio, in a mischievous mood, kicks Jonathan under the table. Jonathan gets angry and upsets the fruit salad. In horror, I watch the pieces of fruit dropping onto my trousers, the juice spilling all over the table, onto the children and on the floor, in a multicolored flood. Vivien gasps in dismay. I get angry at Emilio, the cause of the whole incident, and grab him by the arm. He screeches, then bites me vengefully. All eyes in the cafeteria turn to us. It is a nightmare.

Later, after all the fuss is over, I look back and understand. Emilio and Jonathan were manifesting concretely my and Vivien's emotions. Our feelings and desires are not a private, isolated fact. Whether we like it or not, they propagate and reach those around us in a thousand ways—sometimes evident, but mostly subtle and mysterious. We communicate the way we feel and think not only by what we say and do, but also in our gestures, tone of voice, and whatever mood we emanate. In this way we influence those closest to us, and most of all our children.

Children are capable of feeling clearly and directly our hidden and deepest moods. They respond to our emotions with an intensity and sensitivity greater than our own, because they have no protection. It is paradoxical: They pick up our emotions better than we can. This sensitivity often disturbs them, as they cannot count on the filters and defenses we adults have.

One day Emilio dictates to me a list of all the words that must not be said in his presence. Many are words denoting negative sentiments, such as *sad*, I am *sorry*, What a *pity*. "I want you to be always happy," he says. Of course, Emilio will have to come to terms with negative emotions, but for the time being I must be mindful of the consequences that my inner states can have for him and Jonathan.

Not only do children feel our emotions more intensely than we do, but they also act them out. If children feel rage, they will bite someone or hurl a plate onto the floor. If they feel depression in the air, they will stop eating or wet their bed. They experience our emotions with their whole organism and often express them vigorously and immediately. We, on the other hand, have learned the fine art of self-protection, of imploding, rationalization, mediation, denial.

Children are frank. As in the story of the emperor's new clothes, they will say quite candidly what we adults are afraid to express. Emilio once said to some lingering guests, "Why don't you go home?" Another time, when a man lit a cigarette in a shop, he shouted, "You horrible man, cigarettes are bad!" And when a lady with some facial hair got on our bus, he exclaimed, "Look, Daddy, a lady with a beard!"

It is embarrassing. There often is, in all of us, a contrast between what we feel inside and how we would like others to see us. We adults manage to conceal and control our most private feelings. But a child will put them on display for us. Why is it that every parent is embarrassed when her child throws a tantrum in public? Not only because at that moment she is the center of attention, or that she fears disturbing others or being judged. It is because she feels exposed, afraid that her most private life is coming out in the open.

Capable of sensing our unexpressed emotions, and mostly free of inhibitions, our children manifest the most intimate aspects of our existence in the theater of life. There on stage they act out the whole range of our inner states. Their dramas illustrate exactly and ruthlessly our most intimate psychic life.

Talk about airing dirty laundry in public. We are dealing here with baring our innermost feelings—any time or place: at home or in the supermarket, at the house of friends or on the freeway, at church or in a restaurant. We are publicized. Our children, a piece of our biological makeup, have taken on a life of their own. They live and recite our very being, showing everyone that which we really are, and with an extraordinary facility and lack of inhibition, as no one else could do.

To be sure, each child has his own feelings and inner world, his own unique personality. Nevertheless, in the early years a child is in a kind of symbiosis with us. His unconscious and ours are one.

It is a Zen technique to show concretely another's way of being, which would otherwise remain unmanifest. In a famous anecdote, a Zen master invites a disciple to tea and then pours tea into a cup that is already full. The cup overflows, flooding the table. "Just as this teacup could not take any more tea because it was already full, so you cannot receive my teaching as long as you are full of your own ideas," says the master.

Our children unintentionally do the same as this master. They continually show us how we think and feel. They yell, throw tantrums, jump for joy, smile, sleep soundly, have nightmares: all that is what we are.

For a time Emilio is very irritable. The slightest opposition makes him explode. Yet he really has everything he could want. Every day Vivien and I spend a lot of time with him and show him our love in exactly the same way as when he is happy and serene. What is going on? Of course, all children have such difficult periods, moments of crisis in their development. This time, however, is different. I realize that this irritability is coming from me. It is a period in which I get up very early, having slept no more than five hours, and I am irritable. I manage to hide it, but it lies beneath the surface of all my states of mind. In order to gain more time for my interests and activities, I cut back on sleep. The consequences show up in Emilio. He senses my irritability and holds it up clearly in front of me: This is what you are. When I start sleeping a little more, the irritability disappears. I am more rested, and Emilio is more serene. It is quite simple: Living in symbiosis with a nervous organism makes you nervous.

Sometimes it happens dramatically. When Vivien is

expecting our second child, we are worried. The baby may not be developing as much as he should—or so we are told. One morning Vivien returns from the gynecologist. She is upset, and I am, too. We later find out that all is well, but right now we are left with our anxieties, which loom over the atmosphere around us. A little later, Emilio, running along the footpath, stumbles and hits his head on an iron gate. We take him to the hospital, where they dress the wound. To this day a tiny scar on Emilio's forehead reminds us of our collective worry.

Luckily, emotional resonance works in a positive way, too. There are days when I feel well and in harmony with everyone, when everything seems right, and the children reflect my serenity. On one such day of happy, harmonious play, fluid and free of tensions, Emilio said to me before going to sleep, "Today you get ten out of ten."

Our values can also be played back to us theatrically. I happen to be critical of our consumer society—except when I take part in it. One evening I bring home a present for Emilio. He had asked me to bring him a sheet of colored paper to use in a collage. For fear of not choosing the right one, I return with seven. My doubts are confirmed: None of them is the one he had in mind.

Emilio is therefore unsatisfied, the disappointment

becomes discontent, which in turn becomes frenzy: "I want more presents! Buy me more presents!" With the inexorable crescendo of a Greek tragedy, the scene develops into a huge tantrum, complete with kicking, screaming, hurling of objects. I see this child, whom I have showered with too many presents, violently demanding more, as if it were his right. I see before me, in concrete form, the result of my true if unconfessed philosophy, that material possessions can make us happy, help us resolve our problems, lift us out of our depression. It is an ideology I have always opposed, but in an undeclared way have often practiced. The result of this philosophy is now in front of me, in the form of a child angrily craving new possessions.

When Emilio's little brother is born, I think that it is normal for a child to be jealous of the new arrival—so everybody around me keeps telling me. Everyone expects some jealousy, and soon enough, it starts to happen: dangerous little pranks like putting plasticine in the baby's mouth, small health problems, various regressions.

But does it have to be like that? Common expectations, opinions, and anxieties have always raised my suspicion. How big a part do we adults play in generating these problems? Are they really inevitable?

I am convinced that we unconsciously transmit our ideology about love. We regard love as if it were a cake:

You cannot have the whole, but must divide it, and as it is in scarce supply, you have to compete for it in order to obtain some of what you want. Thus rivalry and conflict are born. Such ideas reach us while we are still in the cradle, and we pass them on to our children. Love is blended with the fear of losing love, or of never having enough.

I become aware of this situation a few nights after Jonathan is born. Emilio has caught a bad cold and wakes up every fifteen minutes because he is not breathing well. I try unsuccessfully to persuade him to accept nose drops so that he will have no more trouble. Every fifteen minutes I rush to console him, hoping it will be the last time and he will let us sleep.

Finally I change tactics. I hold him and start rocking this four-year-old as if he were a baby. Then I put him down and watch him, feeling great love for him and empathy for his difficulty with the birth of his baby brother. I place a hand on his chest and try to convey the warmth and abundance of my love for him. Something in me is changing, and I can love this child in a new way, serenely and without contradiction. Even though I shall have to divide my time between the two, I shall not have to divide my love, which is beyond mathematics, and cannot be sectioned. Emilio falls soundly asleep after a few minutes and wakes up in the morning regenerated and happy. Maybe the problem was not his blocked nose but my struggle with the intricacies of love.

This business of others matching our expectations is subtle, intriguing, somewhat alarming. Is it true that people tend to become what we think of them? And what do they think of us? These are the most useful questions to ask oneself. For instance, I find myself thinking of my wife as someone who is always late. Every time we have to go somewhere together, I wait. While waiting, I get irritable and my thought that she is always late is reinforced. Her lateness, and my irritation, are a well-established family ritual. So next time I decide to perceive Vivien as somebody who may or may not be late. We will see. I keep the thought entirely to myself. And, as if by magic, she is punctual. Are our thoughts communicated in subtle ways, for instance by our facial expressions and gestures? Or is it telepathy? I do not know, but I see this happening again and again. Not always (luckily), because other people have a life and a will of their own. The time after that, Vivien is again late, and we are back to the old ritual. But then another time she is again punctual, and I find that as I free myself of my old thoughts about her, I feel better even when she is late. Because if I think somebody always keeps me waiting and will do so for the rest of my life, I feel much worse than if I leave her the space for changing.

One of my colleagues is warm and friendly when the two of us are together, but if we are in a meeting, he will start making negative remarks, sabotage, change the subject. Everyone knows he will do that, and he does it every time. We expect him to be that way, and invariably he fulfills the prophecy. So I decide to hold a different image of him: He may or may not sabotage. . . . Unfortunately, it does not work this time, because he behaves according to script. I notice, however, that at least I feel differently about him. He does not appear a two-dimensional caricature, but rather like a three-dimensional, complex, living human being. I know that he is not merely as he appears at this moment, and that helps me—even though the meeting itself is a disaster. We are not responsible for other people's behaviors, but we are responsible for how we feel and think about them.

It is in the nature of my work as a therapist that, when I give sessions, I notice how my inner world affects others. If I am bored, distracted, irritated, my clients will revert to their usual hang-ups. If I perceive them as they perceive themselves, we will not make any progress—we are locked in the same prison. But if I see them as they could become, if I hold open my views about them, change is more likely to occur.

I see that what happens externally is—partially, at least—a result of how I am inside. The events that go on each day in the noisy, concrete world around me are a condensation of my silent, fleeting, subjective world. They are different forms of the same substance, just as the watery vapor of a cloud and a raging torrent are forms of the same water.

This realization has major consequences. It gives me an extra reason to take care of how I feel. Am I serene? Am I giving the best of myself? Am I happy? Of all thoughts, this last is the most selfish. But it is also the most altruistic, because my well-being, my freedom, my spiritual growth express themselves with inescapable punctuality in my own children.

It is a relief, too. I no longer have to worry whether what I do is selfish or altruistic. It is both. I ask instead which states of mind and which actions are the most effective in creating the greatest happiness and freedom for all. And then I work toward them.

Truth

The cake looks delicious. It has just come out of the oven and the aroma tantalizes me. It is a black cherry tart. However, it is full of sugar and fat and white flour, and I am with Emilio. I must not set a bad example. Vivien and I want to look after his teeth and teach him good eating habits.

But the tart is tempting, my desire irresistible. Well, why should I renounce such a pleasure? Maybe I can buy the tart on the sly and give Emilio a whole wheat bread roll. That will distract him. After my purchase, holding the tart, I turn my back to him and begin eating it, trying not to be seen. Emilio notices straightaway and energetically asks for it. "Hey, that roll is really good, isn't it?" I say, meanwhile gulping down the tart as quickly as possible. Emilio is not interested in the roll. He throws it on the ground with disdain.

Caught red-handed! Had I been alone, I would have eaten the pastry in peace. In Emilio's presence, I have no choice but to see myself the way I am. I can't pretend, I can't lie, I can't tune out. And so it goes on every day with my children. With them around, it is impossible to live in fantasy: I am confronted with the truth of what I am.

Jonathan uncovers in the shopping bag a pineapple almost as big as he is. He carries it to me with great effort, places it before me, looks at me, and says, "Umm." I am tired. I have no desire to cut it up and prepare it for him. He has already eaten. I say, "Try to eat it." Angrily, Jonathan pushes it to me, saying, "Knie" (knife). Once again I have been caught cheating. My kids show me all the little lies and inconsistencies with which I try to navigate the rocky reefs of our daily life.

Sometimes the truth announces itself in a moment of drama. We are having a family argument. Emilio has thrown one of his tantrums. I run after him and reproach him, and so does Vivien. Emilio, in his anger, throws over a couple of chairs. We are all in turmoil. Then we hear a tiny voice. "Oh, dear!" It is Jonathan, in his high chair, hands on his cheeks, watching us, horrified. Where have I ended up? We three, taken by surprise, stand still as statues. We look at each other and, a little embarrassed, start laughing. Quite a revelation, seeing ourselves through the eyes of a toddler.

It sometimes seems to me that I am looking in a mirror. This happens because my children imitate me. I know that children learn by imitating. They copy our gestures, our behavior, our voices. Although original and unique, they at times move about like small replicas of us. We see ourselves in them, the way we scratch our heads when thinking about a problem, the way we swear, the way we hold a telephone, the way we eat.

We have seen how children can act out our own deepest emotions and fantasies. At a more superficial level, they mirror us. A mirror is neutral, direct, revealing, and also a little eerie. It shows us what is, without making comments and interpretations. By doing so, it tells us something about ourselves that we do not know, or maybe know but prefer not to know. It is a strange and disquieting faculty: A mirror seems to have a life of its own over which we have no power. The same happens with children: They can be our mirrors, and show us what we are. Perhaps we had not realized it before, and we are genuinely surprised. Or we knew it all along, but we did not want to admit it to ourselves.

Truth can cause discomfort. I remember how Dante Alighieri, in his *Divine Comedy*, has to climb Purgatory in order to reach Heaven. But to enter Purgatory he has to climb three steps that lead to a portal. The first step is white—you see things as they are, with no filter. The second step is gray and broken and represents the shock and uneasiness that come from absolute honesty. But if we can overcome the discomfort of this second step, we move on to the third step, which is red—the release of energy and vitality. While I may not be climbing all the way to Heaven, I recognize the relevance of Dante's metaphor.

Truth—seeing what I am, not what I would like to be—makes me uneasy. And, once more, it helps me find the precious virtue of humility. Not only can I not do all I want to do, I am not the way I thought I was. There is an earthy wholesomeness in humility. I may not reach as high as I would like, but my foundations are firmer. Now I know where I stand.

Children are funny when they imitate grown-ups. But when we look closer, we don't find them quite so funny. We realize we are looking at ourselves.

One day I accidentally drop a piece of paper. Emilio immediately points his finger at me accusingly, turns red in the face, and angrily exclaims, "You are not to do that! Pick it up at once!" A rather comical picture, this child all heated up like a little preacher. Then I realize: That is the way I talk to him, my finger admonishing, when he throws things on the floor. I am the preacher!

However embarrassing, revelations like these are never humiliating. I never feel belittled, merely reappraised. There is always a touch of involuntary humor that helps me see more accurately who I am.

I am putting Emilio to bed. The light is off. It is late, really time for bed. I tell him a story, having first promised only one. Once it is finished, sure enough, comes the request, "Tell me another story."

"Emilio, we said just one, then to sleep."

Now comes the surprising response, in a voice that cuts through the darkness. "Tell me another story or I will give you a kick in the pants."

A fine piece of blackmail. Where did this child (always treated with respect and love, never slapped or menaced) learn to threaten? From me, of course. Hadn't I said a short while before: "If you don't go to bed straightaway, there will be no story"? Yes, I find out that threats are part of my interaction with my children and that they are inherent in many of our social relations, albeit more embellished. If you don't pay the electricity bill, no more light; do not exceed fifty miles per hour, otherwise you will get a fine; behave properly or you will be in trouble.

Emilio rocks his chair backward yet again and I tell him not to. He keeps doing it, falls, and hurts himself slightly. "Serves you right," I say. A few days later, I knock my shinbone while hurrying to get into the car.

While I am still jumping about with pain, I hear a clear voice from inside the car saying, "Serves you right." Added to the pain in my leg is the surprise. This is about what I am. Well, then, I must be sadistic. At the moment of another's pain, I triumph and prove I was right after all. My child mirrors me most faithfully.

Truth liberates us. We usually carry about a distorted image of ourselves. On this point, psychologists are in agreement. Our inner world is like a dictatorial regime in which propaganda takes the place of truth. We represent ourselves the way we would like to be seen, suppressing the data we do not like. For this reason seeing our own photograph or hearing our voice recorded often surprises and perhaps irritates us, at times even disturbs us. We really preferred the illusion. That is exactly what happens to me in living with my children.

With young children, naive and unsophisticated as they are, lies make life simpler. A mother and her child are at the park. The mother wants to go home, the child wants to stay and digs her heels in. The mother tells her, "The big bad wolf is coming to eat up all the children." The child immediately acquiesces. Is it right to gain obedience by trickery?

I know only too well the discomfort I feel when caught in the act of lying. Emilio, two years old, wants fish sticks. There are still some left in the freezer, but I don't want him to have them, as he has eaten a lot of them already. Still, he remembers, and he wants. After offering him other foods without success, I tell him, "There are no more left. You have eaten them all," whereupon Emilio points to the freezer and says, "See no more left."

He wants to verify. A few more evasive tactics on my part, and then I am forced to open the freezer. There they are, the fish sticks, in all their glory, the Holy Grail of the kitchen, won over from the hands of the impostor: the vanquished Daddy. And how does Dad explain himself? Most pathetically: "Goodness, how absentminded of me! I thought they were finished, but there are still some left."

I have no idea what Emilio is thinking. He seems to be interested only in the fish sticks, and not, as we adults would be, in accusing or claiming triumph. Still, I feel exposed in my lying. And even if I had gotten away with it, I should not have felt much better. Telling lies to your child over a long period of time causes a wall to be built that, in the end, bars all communication. I see that deceit can become the path of least resistance, not merely for fish sticks, but for any aspect of life or of ourselves. Just as I conceal prohibited food in the freezer, so I end up hiding myself.

For adults this is a way of life. For children it is a scandal. I remember when I was a child and went to the dentist for the first time, how I was fascinated by his equipment: drills, lights, buttons, jets of water, and other instruments. The dentist, with a certain professional pride, said to me, "I bet when you grow up you will be a dentist like me." My mother, who was standing there, chimed in, "Just think, you will be able to play as much as you like with these lovely gadgets." I liked the idea and as soon as I was outside the door told my mother, "Yes, I think I will be a dentist when I grow up." My mother replied, "Oh, no! Think what a disgusting job, messing around all day in people's mouths!"

The image of a life full of salivating mouths was enough to change my mind. But what upset me was her unexpected switch. My mother, who of all people made a cult of truth, ten minutes before had said that dentistry was a wonderful profession. Now she was saying the opposite. The grown-ups' world, then, must be a factory for falsehoods.

The contradictions between what we say and what we do are most evident to the eyes of a child. I explain to Jonathan that we cross the road when we see the little green man in the traffic lights, not when there is the little red man. Jonathan is very amused. At each crossing he starts yelling with glee, "Little red man! Little green man!"

But one day I am in a hurry and I cross while it is

red. He is angry and confused. It is hard for me to explain my inconsistency. Another time, I tell Emilio he must not drink water straight from the bottle, and not long after he catches me doing it. Taken by surprise, I mutter some words of excuse, before we both burst out laughing.

When our actions belie our words, it is as if we were loosening the bolts in a machine. Sooner or later the mechanism breaks down. We need to check ourselves now and then. So far the inconsistencies my children have noticed are lightweight. But in the years to come they will begin to see the deeper, more philosophical ones. I can sense that there will be no way out, I will no longer be able to hide.

Let us return to the present. I know that my voice can either ring true or false. If I am unsure, Emilio feels it. One day I tell him, "You are the one who really made me feel what love is." When I start the sentence I believe it, but by the end I realize I don't. I had also learned to love before. Emilio looks at me suspiciously, then says, "Do all dads say those things?"

Another time, in a crowded place, we lose sight of each other for a few seconds, and I find Emilio screaming in panic. Later, when we talk about it, Emilio admits he is afraid of being abandoned. I reassure him, "Don't worry, I will never leave you!" I am sincere in saying it, but even while speaking I remember that one day I will leave him—when I die. Anything but reassured, Emilio responds, "You never know what may happen."

I believe children have antennae that tell them whether we are sincere or not. Thus they teach us to be like they are: frank and true. How good it feels to be a hundred percent sincere!

When we are true we are also natural. We do not need to say things more than once. We understand each other immediately. Comments are not necessary. Our words are like an arrow to the target.

Let us take a basic kind of communication: two people saying that they love each other. When our children let us know in their own way that they love us, it is a crystal-clear message—not a word, not a gesture too many. And no sentimentality. We adults instead tend to speak to each other with much elaboration. If we communicate like this to children we often invade them. Since children have a great need of physical contact, and since they evoke enormous affection in us, it is natural for us to want to kiss and cuddle them. However, they know when enough is enough. I have noticed that many children struggle free and run away when their parents attempt to hug them.

Before having children, there was more time for illusion. In some unspoken way, I felt I was special, one day I would do something important, and would claim the admiration of many. It was not an explicit fantasy, rather a mental attitude.

Since I have had children, there is no time for this fiction. I do not feel so special anymore. I am a parent like all the others. With horror, I discover banality. I recognize that I am one of the many. I will not have the time to do all I want—death is nearer every day. Perhaps I shall not go down in history after all.

Those thoughts depress me. Then, however, I realize that this is the way it is, whereas before it was all fantasy. Once again I feel truer. My outlines are sharper, the world out there is clearer, my job, hour by hour, is in focus.

Maybe I feel more fragile. Yet also stronger. Every day with my children I encounter the qualities of love, innocence, beauty. But not one of these meetings would have any value if there were not a strong baseline. Now I know there is that base. Now I am learning to be honest with myself.

The Couple

We are at the railway station, in the waiting room. Three-year-old Emilio cries, "Love! Love!," trying to make us understand that he wants me and Vivien to embrace each other. Though we are embarrassed, we comply, right there, in front of the bored travelers. But we are too inhibited for Emilio. "More love," he says. "More love!" With some reserve, we obey, but it is still not good enough. Emilio keeps insisting, and when at last he is satisfied with our efforts, he squeezes in between us to make a "love sandwich."

Inhibition in front of other people is the furthest thing from his mind. Why on earth should anyone be ashamed of loving? Most important for him is that we, his parents, love each other. How does this child feel, sandwiched between our bodies? I imagine he feels wonderfully secure. Snuggled in the warmth between the two who love him most, he knows that between us affection flows abundantly. He knows all is well. It must be a great feeling.

Perhaps such an idyllic portrait of family love is asking too much. At the beginning of the new millennium, the family is not doing too well. The once enormous tribe of grandparents, aunts and uncles, cousins and friends, has disappeared, and the smaller, nuclear family has taken its place. The institution of marriage is getting shakier by the day. The relationship between the sexes is unclear and controversial. Religious faith is fading; family ties are becoming weaker.

I think of another, quite different episode. The four of us all set out one morning from our house in the country for a day in the city. We are fresh and hopeful. When we return in the evening, we are exhausted and furious. Jonathan is screaming, Emilio is picking on him, Vivien and I are bickering with each other or taking it out on Emilio. This is everybody's war against everybody. The car has become a pressure cooker—a symbol of the dreadful predicament of the contemporary family: people obliged to stay together without any escape. I look inside myself for a corner, just a tiny corner, where I may find a little bit of love left. But I cannot find it.

Luckily, this is merely an episode. Vivien and I normally get along well. Yet I know I cannot rest on my laurels. Our children have both improved and worsened my relationship with Vivien. Improved it, obviously, because I feel an immense gratitude to her for having brought these children into the world: the two most beautiful gifts I have ever received. All I have to do to feel gratitude is think about the time of their two births and see her face, exhausted but radiant with joy. I feel we have embarked together on a glorious adventure in the service of two growing children, helping them to become two human beings.

At the same time, however, our relationship has withered. Vivien and I have very little time to be together alone. The intellectual quality of our dialogues has plummeted: "These diapers leak," "Hurry up, the baby is crying. You'd better nurse him!," "Watch that he doesn't spill food on his good clothes!" Every day with the children is full of ordinary tragedies and depressing trivialities. Put any two human beings in this kind of world, and their relationship and their very sanity are at stake.

Let us go back to the railway episode. Emilio wants to see and feel that we love each other. Why? It is clear: The relationship itself between two people creates a human being. We are all the result of a relation between two parents, and this relation lives within us, whether as loving harmony or as a painful wound. The relationship between our parents makes us what we are. This is true in all cases—even in the case of single parents, artificial fertilization, genetic manipulation, uterus hiring, and sperm banks. Even when one partner is absent, he or she contributes to defining the relation. It is as simple as that: We are born from the relationship between two people.

We can compare this relationship to a vegetable garden. If the soil is fertile and well cultivated, the vegetables will thrive. But what if the garden is full of poisons? A child feels the relationship between her parents with her entire being. If that relationship is polluted, the poisons circulate in her organism. If the atmosphere is chaotic, the child will grow in disharmony. If it is full of insecurities, she will live in anxiety.

It has taken time, but I have finally realized that my relationship with the children passes through my relationship with my wife. I cannot have a good rapport with them if I do not have a good rapport with her. Of course, our relationship as husband and wife has independent value and would be important even if there were no children. But the presence of children makes every issue more concrete, more evident, and more urgent. I have at times forgotten this point. I have become too confident. Knowing full well that we were fine together, I let things be. I left the vegetable garden to itself. I concentrated on the children. Gradually I became a ghost to Vivien, and she became one to me.

On top of it all, Emilio wants to have his say. He wants Vivien and I to love each other, but in his mind, the center of our relationship is his most illustrious and honorable self. One day he and I are talking about his mother and me. I tell him how different our life was before he was here, how we loved each other even then, and had more time to be together. Then I add that one of the next evenings Vivien and I will go out together—an absolute novelty—without him and without Jonathan, because we also like to be together in that way. Emilio's eyes widen with astonishment. Then comes the anger at such effrontery. He cannot conceive the possibility of a happy relationship between Vivien and me that does not involve him.

Luckily I come to my senses before it is too late. It happens like this: The children take so much of my free time that the only time left for me to read, think, write is very early in the morning. I start getting up at five-thirty. Yet the children wake up earlier and earlier. Like an army invading enemy territory bit by bit, they claim new spaces. I start getting up at five, four-thirty, four. This means that by the time the evening comes, I am in a coma. And the evening, when the two children are in bed, is the only time when Vivien and I can be together. The result: Vivien doesn't have a husband, but a zombie.

If someone were to ask me, I would say that Vivien is more important to me than writing. But I would be cheating: I keep the best part of my day for writing and give however little is left of me in the evening to her. Morning is my haven, all that is left of my freedom. I need it vitally. I tell myself that if they take that time away from me, I will go mad.

However, I am depressed. Something doesn't make sense here. My writing gets stuck. In the end I realize what I know but have not wanted to admit to myself: My priorities are wrong. I choose to get up later. With a sense of panic I decide to give up the time for thinking and writing. Letting go: What a lesson that is. Letting go even of that which seems to be vital. I give back to my wife a husband who is not a ghost.

Immediately I feel good again. I rediscover a forgotten treasure. I see that the people in our life are much more precious than any interest or activity. My writing flows again, and I end up finding time for it. Once I change my priorities in my own mind, I can even get up early in the morning without becoming exhausted later in the evening.

Another, subtler change also occurs. The relationship between Emilio and Vivien suddenly improves. It was not exactly bad, but I did not like the way he was often rude to her, or sometimes spoke with me as if Vivien did not exist. He would ignore her, as you could expect from some callous chauvinist. I strongly disliked it but did not know what to do about it, other than preaching. Then I realized: Without knowing it, Emilio was showing me my own attitude toward Vivien. It was I, not he, who was treating her like a shadow. Fortunately, I found out. Every time I change my inner attitude toward Vivien, Emilio's outward ways with her also change.

To renounce. In this age of righteous self-assertion and clamorous demands, what an unpopular necessity, and yet what a noble art. When we have a family, that is our inevitable destination—whether we like it or not. It is a universal truth. We have to renounce time, energy, projects, money, even cherished theories, to give more to the family we have created. Not all of them, but a part. The choice is not between giving up and not giving up, but between doing it in good grace or resisting every bit of it. Yes: I have to give up pieces of my preexisting life because of my wife and children. If I do it grudgingly, I will resent my family. I will see them as the main obstacle between myself and freedom. But if I give up willingly, if I don't hold on tightly and let go lightly, I realize that they, my wife and my children, are even more important than that which I am renouncing—be it time or energy or projects or whatever—and this realization makes me feel them much closer to me. It helps me see how overwhelmingly precious they are to me.

Now I get a clearer picture. First of all, I understand

even better how being in a family pitilessly shows up all my problems and limitations. They are all there in front of me. Before, they were vague, intangible. I could pretend they did not exist. Now I cannot cheat anymore. My hang-ups used to be an unpleasant phantom. They have become an embarrassing reality.

If I am depressed, my depression is there for all to see. If I am irritated, my irritation is an extra guest at the dinner table. If I am confused, I see my confusion appear in my loved ones. My mind is public. There is no privacy in the family. Every day I see my thoughts out in front of me, as if on stage. Dynamic and potent, they change reality and color the atmosphere, they are reflected in my words and actualized in my actions.

I also see that I can learn to accept. I had long ago discovered how easy life becomes when we just accept what is. Wanting the universe to fit our preferences: What a thankless job! Hoping people will change: What a waste of energy! Trying to make them behave as we want: A sure way to generate anger. I rediscover the art of acceptance. Vivien is Vivien, the children are the children. That is all. I do not add hopes that they behave in a certain way, or recriminations when they do not.

I renounce all models of how they should be. Why on earth should my models constrain them? And yet this is what we so often do to others, as if they had signed a contract with us to be a certain way. But they are not responsible for our projections about how we want them to be. Our models of how they ought to be are our own creation. And even if we let them know, why should they in any way be bound? And why would we put them on trial for not doing so?

Little by little, I become more available to my family. My center of gravity is right here: with this person, my wife, my child, in front of me—not in the distant land of hope. This I have learned by being with my children, but I must not reserve it only for them. This is a skill that may be taken anywhere. It is at the basis of every relationship.

I find that if I really love a person, I must never take her for granted. Every relationship, especially that with my wife, needs renewal. Like the vegetable garden, I have to look after it. To care. Unfortunately, I have a tendency to express criticism but withhold appreciation. Why? Perhaps it is because I hope to correct others with my criticism and wonder why I should express appreciation if all is going well and we all know it. If I make it a point to remember, finding qualities to appreciate is easy. I nurture the vegetable garden.

The great enemy here is laziness. The line of least resistance is yielding to habit in thought, feeling, and action. I realize it one day when, in a conversation with Vivien, I tell her that I think children should wear shorts even in cold weather, as I did when I was a child, because that maximizes exposure to the sun and vitamin D absorption. "I know that," she says factually. "You have already told me." The truth is that I have already told her more than once. And this is not middle-age loss of memory: I remember telling her. I just don't make the effort to find something new to say. That is when I realize there are various attitudes I can take that will turn my wife into a mummy—at least in my eyes: (a) Make predictable statements; (b) do not share what is most exciting for me—discoveries, insights, coincidences; (c) engage in rituals: repeat again and again the same behaviors together; and (d) take her for granted—as if I already knew everything that she will ever be and do. What horror. I decide that every day I will find something puzzling or mysterious about her, or I will say something I have never said before, or I will share a piece of my experience really important to me.

I like to recall the most beautiful moments, when my relationship with Vivien was new. The freshness of those times helps me find the original inspiration in our relationship. Contrary to what many think, I believe that falling in love is not a kind of folly. On the contrary, it is the best moment for two people, when they see all their possibilities open before them, when they touch the essence and beauty of love. From that moment on, everything risks becoming dimmer and duller.

Falling in love: That is where we can find what is truest.

The idea that the hard knocks of life are the only reality and that the freshness of falling in love is a delusion seems to me moralistic and pessimistic. I can see, with my mind's eye, our best times together: our first walk, the trip to Spoleto, the marriage proposal on a September afternoon, Vivien at the airport on a rainy day, a concert when she was pregnant with Emilio, Jonathan's very first breast-feeding. Those are the origin, the source. In the place where everything is okay, nothing is tainted with the paranoia of everyday life. Once in a while it is good to return to the source. And drink the pure water of the fount.

In these ways—awareness and control of thoughts, availability, acceptance, appreciation, returning to the beginnings—I gradually change the circuits in my mind. I feel different. The mirror that was clouded can once again reflect light.

Gratitude

In line at the supermarket checkout, Emilio and I hear a child screaming. The child's brother and sister are there, too. The brother soon starts crying, and the sister, not much older, follows suit. The mother, a robust, stern woman who looks like she has fought her share of battles, immediately whips out three chocolate bars and shoves one into each of the three mouths. End of crying. The children munch away. Now they are quiet.

Emilio watches the whole scene in silence. In our family, while allowing exceptions, we try not to fill ourselves with chocolate and other sweets. Emilio, on an empty stomach, grows pensive. We leave the supermarket. Half an hour later, on the way home, a pained cry rings out: "I wanted a chocolate bar, too!"

An ordinary sweet. But enough to penetrate the psyche of a child and ruin his morning if he cannot have it. I am dismayed: I would like to surround my children with a world that is beautiful and stimulating, wholesome and totally safe. It is an impossible task, I realize. Children are immersed in a world beyond our control.

I know about the long-term dangers of a diet based on chocolate bars. Yet that is small stuff compared to other, more insidious risks. For example: While I am fairly liberal in sexual matters and would like to remove many of the barriers to sexual freedom, I shudder at the pornographic photographs displayed in magazines, visible to all, including my children—obscene pictures of crassness and vulgarity. A disgraceful initiation into sexual life.

I would also prefer that my children are not hypnotized by countless images, violent and in bad taste, that television uses to promote a materialist, dull-witted way of thinking. Like extraterrestrials that invade our planet and mingle with the population, TV images enter the minds of children and merge with their everyday life, leading them to mistake illusion for reality. An entire generation of children now talks like TV personalities. Our sons, for the time being, are not interested in television, because we hardly watch it. However, since the tube is part of the culture we breathe every day, I know the time will come when it will make fiercer claims on their attention.

And what about pollution? When I tell Jonathan we are going to the sea and we will play on the beach, he straightaway asks me, "Will there be any tar?" He remembers one afternoon we spent on a beach. Afterward we had to clean the black stuff off his body. And noise pollution; Emilio, at about four years of age, goes through a period when he bursts into tears at any sharp sound.

Now I realize that I have brought two children into a polluted, violent, sometimes horrid world. I know there are millions of viruses floating around in the air, riding on buses, making their homes in cafés and post offices: aggressive viruses capable of entering my children's bodies, attacking their blood and nervous system. I know the air my children breathe, the water they drink, the food they eat are full of poisons. I have read that, even before conception, more than a hundred substances can mutate the genetic makeup of a child, causing grave physical and mental defects. And all this happens in a world overcome by hunger and war and filled with turmoil and catastrophes.

Other dangers are lurking. The world is full of people brimming with kindness and goodwill. Being a parent has helped me see this. But dangerous people also abound. People who may be nasty and harmful to my children, even without wanting to be. I thought about this once when going to the fruit vendor—a man who is warm and cheerful in the morning but drunk and de-pressed at the end of the day. As he serves us one evening, interrupting himself over and over again with discourses on the shocking state of things, he notices Emilio. "What a lovely child! Here, have a strawberry. You like strawberries, don't you? Have an apricot. Do you like apricots? Have an apple! Have this chocolate." Emilio's hands are loaded with these presents. He does not know what to do. He looks at me.

I don't know what to do, either. I do not want to of-fend this kind man. But he is starting to be invasive. Now he begins stroking Emilio's cheek. "What a lovely child!" he repeats, with insistence and a touch of bois-terousness. Finally, we thank him, leave hurriedly, and as I drive back I have to explain to Emilio what it means to be drunk.

Fortunately, the fruit vendor is harmless. Emilio has not run into any danger. So far, the greed and the evil of the world have not touched him or Jonathan, except in remote ways. Evil, till now, has been a possibility, not a reality. Yet this episode makes me think. Looking at the rough hands of the fruit vendor touching Emilio's innocent face, I think of how many hands would be able to harm him.

My kids are indeed largely out of my sphere of in-fluence. From the moment of their conception, they have entered a game with its own rules. This makes me anxious. I realize how incomplete, unjust, and precarious life is. I see that a life has a script of its own, independent of my own plans. I am not omnipotent. Control is an illusion. I must drop the ideal of perfection and limit myself to doing my best: a more modest, but truer goal. I feel humbler.

Humility leads to surrender. My children do not belong to me. At first this notion feeds my fears. But later it evokes in me a greater capacity to trust. I could increase the controls, erect protective barriers around them. But that would only make my children weak and immature. Something in me has to change. I start nurturing the idea of acceptance.

Acceptance of evil is out of the question. Rather, it is a matter of accepting a universe in which evil also exists. Pain exists. Death exists. It is my duty to protect my children, but life, in all its mystery and variety, is inexorable. Emilio and Jonathan are independent beings, with their own resources and their own destiny.

Accepting means eliminating all useless mental efforts. I am not responsible for everything. I do not waste time condemning myself, fearing the worst, imagining catastrophes. I face life day by day, as best I can. Reality, when seen without the filter of fantasy and superfluous emotion, is clearer. Being able to accept, I feel freer.

I am part of a process that is bigger than I am, and

it goes on autonomously. It is as if, seated on a 747, I had always thought I was the one in charge of flying it. I had worked hard at piloting, angry when the plane did not obey. I had studied the route, tensing when I thought I was not following the right course. Now I realize someone else is in the cockpit. It is a great relief.

Of course I do not know who is the pilot. In my most optimistic moments, I believe it to be a superior intelligence. I think it is God. Then, when I realize that I do not have complete control over my children, I feel I am entrusting them to God. What more could I hope for? They are in good hands.

My optimistic phases, however, alternate with darker ones. I look at my children's eyes, at the starry sky, at fields of wildflowers in bloom, and my faith grows and glows. But I glance at the newspaper, and life appears an inexplicable, sinister affair—surely not guided by a superior intelligence. Perhaps the plane is piloted by a madman. Yet even in these moments I manage to have trust. I recall that we human beings are the result of an immemorial struggle for survival. We are strong, ingenious, exceptionally resourceful. We are well equipped. We will make it, and my children will, too.

All I have to do is watch my children at play. They are so full of joy and enthusiasm. They run and jump with inexhaustible energy. Every day I am surprised by their intelligence and originality. Like all children, they are curious and have a thousand interests. Even when they throw tantrums and dig their heels in over some silly issue, or fight with each other, they show me that they are prepared to fight the battle to the end. And win.

It is also helpful to see how Emilio deals with evil and death (too early for Jonathan yet). Emilio is opposed to all kinds of abuse and violence. He cannot stand injustice. When the Cat and the Fox trick Pinocchio into believing he can grow gold coins on a tree, Emilio is furious and wants me to stop reading. When he hears of someone setting a mousetrap, he is shocked. If he sees me kill a mosquito, he is outraged. He has even refused to eat meat, saying that he does not want to eat the flesh of any living being.

At five years old, Emilio deals with the problem of death by constructing his Spirit Machine: a complex collage made of colored paper, patterns, arrows, and knobs on a screen. It is possible to make anyone we choose appear on this screen, not only during the person's life, but also after his death, and even in past and future incarnations. In this way Emilio can tune in to his grandmother, who died recently, make her appear on the screen, and talk with her. By creating a kind of spiritual Internet, Emilio defeats his anxiety about death.

Though Emilio's methods seem naive to my adult eyes, his strong sense of justice, his desire not to harm, his resourcefulness, and his positive stance in the face of death, encourage and strengthen me. I, too, make a decision not to eat meat.

Then optimism wavers again. I look at Jonathan's face: He has just woken up in a bad mood. He looks frightened. His beautiful smile of a few hours ago, when all the world was an earthly paradise to him, is gone. I see in his eyes surprise and fear, as he thinks for an instant that he is alone. I know that suffering may arise at any moment in the lives of my children.

Like all parents, I wish only for the health and happiness of my children. Even a cold or a headache seem unfair to me: How dare they afflict a child so perfect and so beautiful? But no matter how we manage to defend and protect our children, they still suffer. They will grow and become adults who will suffer again and again during the course of their existence and will be subject to pain, decay, and death.

Death, in fact, impends over all life, and with children this threat becomes clearer and more intense. Every parent, at some time or other, thinks of this possibility. In me the thought takes the shape of anxious fantasies. It happens in this way: We did not let Emilio go out and about alone with a babysitter until he was almost five years old. Finally, one day he goes out with an extroverted, self-assured girl. They go to the beach. I make nothing of it at first, but once I realize I have no way of reaching Emilio, I begin to worry. What a fool I was to entrust him to someone I did not know well! What is going to happen?

My fantasies are vivid: He has been run over by a bus. I see the most frightful details of the accident, the blood, the body. I even imagine how alone and abandoned he must have felt in his last moments. I imagine our life with Jonathan only. I imagine our pain, our emptiness.

Of course, Emilio comes back from the beach sprightly and cheerful, having enjoyed himself immensely. Pain and misfortune remain as remote possibilities. I understand another fundamental point. The existence of evil, by a curious paradox, makes everything more intense and beautiful. If I watch the sunset over the sea, I can admire its beauty. But if I were to watch it knowing that the next day I would die, its beauty would be even more poignant. An accident miraculously avoided, the healing of an illness, a risk faced and overcome, make us perceive our life in a truer, more intense light.

Seeing the beauty of my children, their innocence— so pure and yet so vulnerable—knowing it will not last, and knowing that they, too, will be touched by the ugliness of life, that they, too, will grow old and die, fills me with horror. At the same time it allows me to have a much deeper appreciation of the happy moments, because they are priceless gifts. I feel gratitude for life. In a way, the pathos of our existence makes its magnificence stand out. What would beauty and love be in a world without pain and death? Hard to imagine, so far away are we from such a condition: I think all beauty would become more banal, all love flat.

Gratitude. So far, this has been the greatest gift of parenthood—gratefulness for having been given the privilege of looking after them. For enjoying the freshness and the beauty of childhood. For the glimpses into wonders I had forgotten. Gratefulness for the blessings of love. Naturally, I don't experience gratitude all the time with my children—far from it. I also feel worry, anguish, rage. But when gratitude occurs, it is profoundly healing, and it radically transforms my personality and view of the world.

If I think that the people I love are subject to misfortune, sickness, and death, I love them all the more. At first my love is anxious. Then it becomes more serene. The certitude of evil and of death draws us near to each other: To know that everything comes to an end, that tragedies in life are inevitable, makes love more vibrant, gratefulness more true.

I remember when Jonathan had not yet been born. It seemed he was not growing enough. A pregnancy can evoke all sorts of anguishing fantasies. Add to that the opinion of experts, and the possibilities multiply. They tell us the baby is not growing as it should. How come? Is he weak, tiny, handicapped, or will a birth defect cause him to die as soon as he is born?

We go for an ultrasound. The doctor very precisely points out all the parts of the future Jonathan: These are the legs, this is the spinal column, the cranium, the little heart beating. Visionary scenes appear on the screen, like landscapes of another planet. This baby is to be born in a few weeks, and we are traveling inside his body: what a prodigious ride! Somehow it is as if we were meeting him. At the end of the journey the words "Everything is okay" bring us wondrous relief.

As I drive back to work at sunset and the first stars appear in the sky, I listen to a piano concerto by Mozart on the radio. Suddenly I feel the presence of the being about to be born. It is not just an idea, I am sure, but a living being as real as this car or this music. I am neither a clairvoyant nor a medium. Yet, just as it happened with Emilio, I perceive the strong, clear presence of my unborn child. Very rarely have I felt so close to a living creature.

The explanation is simple. As I realize more deeply the precariousness of our condition and the possibility of death, my feelings are stirred. A door opens in me to a vast and mysterious world—a door that is usually closed. Maybe it is there to protect me, everybody, from a reality we are not ready to face yet. In this exceptional moment the door opens. I enter, and that permits me, for an instant, to perceive the intangible and, in a more lucid way than ever, to love.

Patience

Jonathan is a little fearful of the slide. Perhaps he has had an unpleasant experience and has become more cautious. He has adopted a new method for playing on the slide: He starts from the bottom, climbs a few steps up, then slides down very slowly. This is just enough for him. Each time he climbs up higher and comes down faster. Every now and again he looks at me, pleased with himself, clapping his hands against the slide as if to say, *I have done it.* I am happy for him.

But now the plot thickens. Other, much older children enter the scene. They want to go down the slide fast, and they don't even notice Jonathan. He goes up, at his own pace; then, seeing these dynamos, he has to come down again and let them slide down. Occasionally, the slide is free for a moment, allowing him to try his luck again, only to find that the older children immediately reoccupy it. He had come very close to mastering it. I know that it means a lot to him to be able to go down the slide. He is gaining confidence, letting himself go. He had been making progress; now it is all lost.

As if that were not enough, two more children have started arguing with each other right next to the slide. Jonathan watches them closely. His rhythm has been completely disrupted. He is puzzled.

I am feeling frustrated. Whenever Jonathan starts climbing, he has to step aside. I notice a sensation of uneasiness mixed with impatience. Just when he is about to take his last step to success, he is interrupted.

I would like to take him to another slide where he can continue his slow, methodical work in peace. Then I realize that would be cheating. Life is chaotic, noisy, at times senseless. To work undisturbed is a luxury. We have to learn to deal with confusion and incompleteness. We both, Jonathan and I, have to learn patience.

One day I am playing with Emilio. This is what we do: He puts a cushion on the floor and lies down on top of it. I have to pretend to be passing by and notice the cushion, but not Emilio. I then have to say, "What is this cushion doing here?," pick up the cushion plus the forty-pound Emilio, put it in its place, and exclaim with great surprise, "But this is not a cushion! This is my son!" For some obscure reason Emilio likes this game a lot. At first, I like it, too. I see him lying down, eyes closed, smiling in anticipation of the exhilarating surprise. "This cushion has a voice, arms and legs, it looks like Emilio . . . wait a minute, it is Emilio!" At the start we are both having fun. But he wants to do it over and over again, and every time it is a big joke for him.

I know repetition is important for a child. That is how children understand, feel reassured, and assimilate. At the end of each go, the enthusiastic, "More!" explodes, and I play again. Nevertheless, after a while I start getting bored and tired. At last Emilio says, "That's enough." What a relief. Maybe we can do something more interesting. I let him choose. But I am in for a surprise: "Let's play the same game again with all the other cushions in the house."

With Emilio and Jonathan, I often find myself doing something all over again. For instance, I put Jonathan to sleep by walking up and down, rocking him to music. It is lovely, if it doesn't last long. But some evenings Jonathan takes ages to fall asleep. I feel I have become a rocking machine. Once upon a time I used to choose the accompanying music. Now he chooses unbearable nursery rhymes, and we have to listen to them hundreds of times. When, finally, I believe him to be asleep, I place him ever so gently and slowly on the bed so as not to wake him up, already anticipating my freedom. But as soon as I put him down, Jonathan yells in outrage, and we are back to square one.

I need patience with these children. I knew that before having them, but I was not fully aware of it till I became immersed in the work of being a father. I need immense patience.

I believe this is our common lot. If we have a family, we will have to face some typical situations millions of times. Saying the same things again and again, being continually interrupted, adapting ourselves to our children's rhythms, accepting disorder and confusion, giving up our plans.

It's enough to create a nightmare world—one that resembles the ordinary world and intersects it, but in which thousands of mechanisms either slow it down or break it down. Not even the most diabolical of minds could have devised such an elaborate method for wearing out our nerves.

If we tackle this world with high hopes and a rigid attitude, we will be in trouble, because it is organized in such a way as to disintegrate, bit by bit, the entire functioning of our lives. Fortunately there is an alternative, perhaps the only one—to see the difficulties as a school in which we can learn the essential virtue of patience.

Patience

I have always been impatient. Just standing in a line or waiting for the elevator are ordeals for me. While waiting at a traffic light, I often think it must be broken, because it never turns green fast enough. And if someone does not immediately understand what I say, I am easily irritated.

That is the way I am. My internal rhythm is fast, and I feel I am always waiting. Being with children is a continuous challenge for me, because I have to learn to go more slowly, terribly slowly. I believe, in theory, that we have to respect their rhythm. In practice, it is just too much. I get impatient and hurry everybody up. Then I realize I am wrong. I have interfered with a subtle process. No one likes being hurried. I am convinced that for children this is a small violation.

It is no coincidence that one of the most common childhood accidents is dislocation of the shoulder, caused by an adult in a hurry pulling a child too hard by the hand. This is symbolic. It is as if we were forcibly pulling children away from their world. And, as always, what we do to others, we do to ourselves. We drag ourselves away from life, from the chance of being in contact with the world.

How often do we hear ourselves saying to a child, "Come on, hurry up! How much longer will I have to wait?" Yet hurry does not belong at all to a child's way of being. Emilio once asked me, "When do the hours finish?"—that is, when does time stop? He meant, I think, When will this racing about finish? When does time end so we can live in peace?

Of course, children have to learn to move about in the world, respect their commitments, be punctual. But the subject here is not what children have to practice—it is what parents can learn.

I, who love lightning speed, now wish to make a eulogy to slowness. I have learned, despite myself, to appreciate the slowness that dilutes time. There are no goals to pursue other than doing what I am doing right now, and I don't have to compete with anyone else. Hurry is often based on fear—the fear of not making it in time. Slowness is not. I can savor every moment, I can at last come to know myself.

Sometimes, when I have surrendered my haste, my desire to get to the point, I have accepted Jonathan's or Emilio's rhythm, and I realize I am attending the School of Patience.

It is a tough but rewarding school. I have learned that patience is not merely a virtue, but an altogether different perception of time. It means that time does not move in a linear fashion, galloping menacingly and then expiring, but an ever-present time, in which I float, freely.

It can happen anywhere: on the street, in play parks, at the train station. Instead of a part of myself being with my children while the other part is struggling and trying to speed up, I am there with my entire self. Patience is a more efficient way of loving.

The first time I confront patience is at Emilio's birth. It takes twelve hours, quite normal for the first baby, but not at all for me. Those twelve hours seem like twelve millennia. As the cervix gradually dilates, the baby has to descend slowly. He has to pass through a corridor that separates him from the world. It is a tunnel only a few centimeters long, but full of different sensations, risks, and perhaps pain. It is an interplanetary voyage. Yet Emilio's speed is only a few millimeters an hour. I am distressed at how slowly everything is happening. It is as if I were living in a slow-motion world, and it is slowing down even more.

Several years later I am taking Jonathan out. He cannot yet walk, so I am carrying him. He looks around, interested in everything. He points to a tree, we go up to it, he touches the bark, fascinated by this strange skin. It is a dry, crumbly bark that peels off easily. I let him do it. He continues, fascinated, touching it, stroking it, turning a piece in his hands, examining it at length.

At first I participate in his wonder. I imagine what bark must look like the very first time. After a while I think he has seen and touched it for long enough and I start to leave. But he protests; he wants to stay. A bit later I try again, but he is still interested. I decide not to interrupt him. I wait while he continues to observe. With a gesture he then indicates that he wants me to take him to another tree nearby. He begins examining its bark, and I hope it will take less time, but this time the investigation takes longer. This is a different bark, thinner and smoother, almost papery. Beneath it, the tree is moist and soft. My arms are tired. I would like to go home. At last Jonathan communicates that he has finished with this second tree. Okay, let's go, then. Oh, no! He wants to return to the previous tree, perhaps to make a comparison, or to do further research.

Suddenly I realize that I must let go of my impatience. While Jonathan touches and observes the first bark again, I try to identify with his way of looking at things. Here we have true understanding. Here we have pure interest. I start to realize what it means to meditate.

I know I must learn to respect my children's rhythms. However, there is still a problem. In order to respect their rhythm, I have to sometimes renounce mine. Each of us has a rhythm, maybe messy, maybe harmonious, but unique as a fingerprint. When we are made to relinquish it, we react with resentment. This is what happens to us with children. It is also what happens when we grow, because we need to realize that there is not only our own rhythm—the rhythm of our desires, impulses, plans—but there are also wider and more harmonious rhythms, such as the ones of nature and of our deeper being. Only in this way can our sense of time expand and, bit by bit, dissolve.

I watch Jonathan, a few months old, while he is nursing. Time does not exist for him. He suckles quietly, enjoying the warmth and the skin contact, the mother's heartbeat, the warm taste of milk. Occasionally he stops and glances around. Or he looks at his mother and smiles. This is perfect peace. There is no before, no after. Why should there be? In a remote and very approximate way I try to participate in this state. As I watch him, I wonder, what else is there to do, if not simply to be?

But what if we are in a hurry, if we have to go somewhere? Right at the moment we are to go out, Jonathan protests. He wants to nurse. Hold everything! How frustrating for us. We shall be late. Emilio is in a bad mood, takes his shoes and socks off, is hungry, eats, and spills food on his shirt. We will have to change his clothes. He then starts playing. To interrupt him will be a problem.

Meanwhile Jonathan nurses. Gradually we, too, begin to feel his tranquillity. Perhaps this is how we are meant to live. You need patience—and patience becomes a relief. A deep-rooted, age-old tension loosens in me. I breathe more freely. Patience, as a door invitingly ajar, opens to the Eternal Present.

These lessons in patience do not remain specific. They extend easily to other areas of my life. Waiting for Emilio to tie his shoe helps me in waiting for a clerk to tidy his desk slowly and methodically before he can answer my questions. Letting Jonathan eat at his own pace helps me in waiting at the shop for a little old lady to finish telling her story to the man behind the counter. I do not tap my foot, I do not tense my muscles, nor do I secretly blame the people who oblige me to wait. I don't panic anymore because I am wasting time. I breathe more deeply and let myself go into a state of serenity where I have nothing to lose. I rediscover patience as a form of kindness and acceptance of other people's rhythms. I awaken to new ways of experiencing time.

"Patience" is derived from the Latin "patire," to suffer. In parenthood, as in all the most fascinating adventures, you have to suffer at times. Every undertaking requires some degree of suffering. Even the most beautiful project, the one that gives us the greatest joy and enthusiasm, sooner or later enters a phase of crisis.

Maybe it is right that it be so. We must be put to the test in order truly to appreciate what is before us, because passion involves our whole being. It is not merely a passing pleasure. It comes up in all projects. Whether we study a language, go on a journey, learn to play a musical instrument, or learn to use the computer, we inevitably arrive at a point where we wonder why we ever took on such a task.

We feel discouraged. At that moment we are not simply encountering our project in its most difficult guise, we are discovering ourselves in our most vulnerable aspect. We are meeting a part of ourselves that we did not know before. We must conquer it, rather than allow it to dominate us.

This is what I have learned in parenthood. I guess almost all parents face times of doubt and discouragement and bewilderment. Certainly this has happened to me, many times over.

Here is an example. Emilio, Jonathan, and I go to the park. We have rented a tricycle for Jonathan, a pair of Rollerblades and a helmet for Emilio, but we still have a fair way to walk before reaching the bike track. Jonathan is in a bad mood and will not walk an inch. I have to carry him. In order to avoid a long argument, I acquiesce. Emilio is in a dreamy state of mind, walks slowly, stopping now and again to ask me the strangest questions. I answer as best I can under the circumstances, while Jonathan strenuously interrupts my conversations with Emilio. The road to the park is tricky because cars drive fast and we have to go through several crossings. I am carrying not only Jonathan but also his tricycle, while Emilio drags his Rollerblades and knee pads in a plastic bag and complains that they are too heavy. We are in a hurry, as we have to take everything back within an hour. When we arrive at last, we find that the tricycle is too big for Jonathan and the Rollerblades are too tight for Emilio. As if this were not enough, it starts raining. There is nothing to do but return to the shop. Another saga with two disgruntled children in the rain.

Right then I feel a mixture of rage and incredulity. How could I end up in such a ridiculous situation? It is not just a passing frustration for me, but a real crisis. This episode, with its painful absurdity, seems to me an accurate symbol of life as a parent.

There is nothing cheerful about this situation. I plunge into depression, not so much for the momentary frustration as for realizing once more how complicated and imperfect life is. Especially for parents.

Yet the depression lifts. I surrender and understand the folly of getting upset. I feel as if I were free-falling, without support and without hope. Is this the satanic laugh of someone falling in the abyss? No. It is a state of mind that, while apparently similar, is in fact the opposite. I recall the whimsical smile I have sometimes seen on the faces of the most seasoned parents. It is a kind of philosophical humor that knows how short life is, how limited are our resources, how grandiose our dreams, how disproportioned our ambitions, how arduous our path—and accepts the lot in good spirit.

Patience

Suffering is part of life. If we can do without it, all the better. But sometimes it is inevitable. Learning to face it, minimize our losses, and perhaps discover new capacities in ourselves, seems to me one of our fundamental tasks. This, too, is patience. This, too, is the art of living.

Intelligence

Emilio has done poo-poo in his pants. He is in the garden, has pulled his pants down, and it has gone just about everywhere. It is a calamity, and his crying expresses utter desperation.

Right at that moment the sun is setting. It is flame-red and spreads a preternatural light over our faces and everything around us. It is a special sunset. As I approach him, Emilio looks at the sun and suddenly says, "Why is the sun red?" The moment his curiosity ignites, desperation vanishes totally. The poo-poo is forgotten. The world is vitally interesting.

Only for a moment, though. A second later Emilio bursts out crying again. Now life is a tragedy again. I, one beat behind him, reply, "The sun is red because its rays pass through the atmosphere."

Still immersed in desperation, Emilio hears me. Meanwhile, I have picked him up and I am carrying him upstairs for a wash. "What is the atmosphere?" I see the interest in his eyes. This subject is important, and he wants to know about it.

The tragedy then makes a reappearance. We have by now reached the bathroom. How humiliating to be covered in shit. I am still one step behind: "The atmosphere is the air all around the earth."

"How come it is all around?" Curiosity returns. In the end, however, crying gets the upper hand.

While washing Emilio, I reflect. I am impressed with Emilio's persistence in asking why, even in the middle of such an unpleasant experience. His exploring mind continually coordinates known facts with new data. It makes hypotheses and verifies them. It always tries to step beyond its own limits. And it never ceases to surprise me.

As an adult, I end up too often using my mind only for making shopping lists and reading the sports page in the newspaper. On the other hand, Emilio, like all children, has a fresh, energetic mind. Even the most ordinary events are hugely interesting for him. In his world, something impressive is always happening. He investigates and experiments all the time.

I find Emilio's questions quite intriguing. Like all children's questions, they are maddeningly difficult to answer, yet perfectly reasonable. I have been jotting them down and placing them in several categories. Here are a few:

Questions about meaning: What is the difference between "rather" and "instead"? What is death? What does "meaning" mean?

Theological questions: "Can God make someone more powerful than Himself?" "Why did God make some things that are useless?" "If I pretend I have a thought in my mind, but do not have anything in my mind, would God think I have something in my mind?" "Can God choose not to exist?"

Psychological and ethical questions: "If I killed Mummy, would you still love me?" "Is it worse to harm a happy person or an unhappy one?"

Hypothetical questions: "What would happen if a car came into our house?" "What would happen if a thief stole all our towels?"

Structural questions: "How come I can't see my own face?"

Historical questions: "Where do you come from?" "What existed before there was life?"

Metaphysical questions: "Is life all a dream?" "What is everything?"

Very often the questions bring up philosophical or scientific problems of great significance. These questions are often too profound and difficult for me. I feel embarrassed. Yet this embarrassment is positive. To be in the company of a curious mind is a tonic for my intellect.

Jonathan is still too young to ask questions. But he is on the ball, too. His curiosity is directed at people. We are on a train. Jonathan begins practicing his specialty: getting to know everybody. He goes up to each individual present, stands in front of him or her, and looks. Perhaps he smiles or waves. And he does not give up till he succeeds in making contact.

As he moves up the carriage, I see the various people through his eyes: the lady dressed in black speaking on her mobile phone, pretending not to see him; the young man who, in order to amuse him, makes animal noises; the shy middle-aged man with thick glasses who does not know how to respond, but in the end smiles; the beaming blonde who leans forward as if to say, More! More!; the student who laughs heartily; the elderly lady smiling, perhaps recalling her own memories.

Jonathan stops and observes. Each person is a different planet. He lands on each planet and explores it. With no inhibition whatsoever, he studies each one, fascinated. This, too, is a form of intelligence. For me, the people on the train were shapeless presences. For him, they are multifarious revelations. Now that I have participated in this interplanetary voyage, I feel richer.

A lively intelligence takes lateral paths. It does not advance by a prearranged logic, but uses any available means. Here is an example. One of Emilio's many passions is riding on the motorized horsey at the supermarket: one dollar for two minutes. As soon as the horse starts to move, Emilio is carried away to a fairyland, his face transformed by amazement. At one point he has an idea: He puts the coin in the slot, but does not mount—he just wants to watch the horse while it gallops. "Emilio, you are wasting the money. The horse is galloping by itself and you are not having fun." In vain. He only wants to observe. People pass by and give us puzzled looks. I feel uneasy.

Emilio is satisfied by studying the situation from a distance. Finally, seeing a little girl walking by and casting an interested look at the horse, he offers her his last coin so she may have a ride.

A fine lesson for me. My mind was traveling along conventional grooves: Insert the money, ride the horse, go home. Emilio's mind has a wider range and different quirks. Having fun, entering a magical world, is only a small part of his activity. He wants to study the up-and-down movement of the horse. Perhaps he wants to understand what it is that gives him the pleasure of galloping. The little girl chances by, and he includes her in the event. These are actions characteristic of a lively mind: to look at the world from a new perspective and to include unforeseen events in whatever one may be thinking or doing.

Children's thought is often divergent. It does not choose the available route, but rather takes the freedom to go where it wants. It does not necessarily use an object or an instrument according to its function, but looks for other ways. For example, Emilio plays with rubber stamps. On one side there is the stamp, and on the other a sponge by which you hold it. Emilio also uses the stamp the other way around: stamping with the sponge. Another example: He immerses an eraser in watercolor, instead of using it to rub out. The results in both cases: colorful, imaginative paintings—more original than if Emilio had been using stamps or rubber in the conventional ways.

The creative mind does not focus merely on what everyone can see, but is curious about the detail that most regard as irrelevant. Children, it seems to me, work this way, too. I have placed an old newspaper on Emilio's easel where he is painting, and on top I put sheets of white paper, one by one. Each time, before I place a new sheet, Emilio looks at the photographs of the people on the newspaper and wants to know their story: the bus driver who rolled into a gorge, how it happened, who went to save him, how they managed to pull the bus out, the present condition of the driver, and so on. This takes us far away from painting, but shows me how an inquiring mind works—by remaining open to a multiplicity of dimensions.

Kids experiment all the time. They throw objects from their high chair to see gravity at work. They play with ice, watching it turn into water—and they observe the transformation from one state to another. They drive you crazy—and they learn how your psyche works, even though they may not phrase it that way.

Mathematics is another big area of research. I love watching my children play with it. I am in a waiting room with Jonathan. Not knowing how to spend the time with him, I roll up some bits of paper into four little balls. Jonathan is fascinated. He takes them one at a time, as if he were counting them, then gives them back to me. I make one disappear, and open my hand showing three balls. Jonathan immediately notices that one is missing. "Ooh!" he says. He waits for me to add it to the other three. After I have done so, he asks me to take it away, then to take away two, then three. There is a lady near us, watching. Jonathan gives her a little ball, then another, then returns to see how many I have left. He continues to play with the various combinations. Half an hour goes by in this fashion.

Emilio wakes up in the middle of the night with a tummyache. I make a chamomile tea and give it to him, one spoonful at a time. With every sip, Emilio remarks: "Tummyache two. Tummyache one. Tummyache zero. Tummyache minus one. Tummyache minus two. Tummyache minus four." The last one seems to me a counting mistake. I say nothing, and Emilio soon explains, "I took two sips instead of one." The numbers decreasing to zero mean the tummyache is going away. The minus numbers mean that the tummy is getting better. Here we are, discovering algebra at two o'clock in the morning.

I also like to see my children exploring the various aspects of the body and its possibilities. Jonathan finds, with some surprise, that he has two hands and two feet. He bends to the ground, supporting himself on his hands, and looks at the world through his legs. He gets me to throw him up into the air, enjoying the feeling of weightlessness. He climbs onto anything he can: He holds my hands and lets himself drop backward, laughing. He asks me to tickle his feet. He does knee bends to the rhythm of music; then he waves his arms in the air like a Balinese dancer. He covers his eyes, thinking I cannot see him anymore, and then uncovers them again. He puts his hands over his ears and then removes them: sound-silence-sound-silence. He practices walking in different ways; like a little soldier, a ballet dancer, a drunken person. He asks me to push him on the swing. He produces all sorts of sounds with his mouth. Walking along merrily one day, he suddenly stops and touches his tongue. He is probably noticing it for the first time in his life.

The imagination. Nearly all children have an extremely prolific fantasy, at least as long as we adults do nothing to repress it. A child can spend days on end inventing story after story as easily as the way we breathe. She enjoys hearing herself tell stories. It seems to me to be almost a basic need.

One day I set about drawing simple labyrinths with Emilio. He is supposed to trace a line from "start" to the center. I think that is all there is to it. But no! We draw labyrinths full of traps and dangers, zigzag labyrinths with multiple exits, ones where we encounter various monsters, people, treasures, hearts, Emilio's friends, ice-cream cones, and so on. They are no longer just puzzles: These are adventures of the mind.

The vitality of the imagination turns up, too, in the use of metaphor. Emilio, like many children between two and six, uses metaphor to interpret situations. Rain is the sky crying. Mummy's nipple is a flower. Broccoli are little trees. The headlights are the eye of a car. The water of a babbling brook laughs. Metaphors show hidden connections and similarities. They reach past the borderline of rational thought. In subtle ways they deepen our understanding of the world.

And what about concentration? We are quick to say children have a short attention span. Perhaps it is more accurate to see their vital attention, sustained by a lively and sparkling curiosity, as directed continuously toward what is new. Even so, children—the very young, too—sometimes have an extraordinary capacity for total absorption.

Jonathan, eight months, finds a plastic bottle. He takes it in his hands, examines it from many angles, lifts it to his mouth, puts it down, and watches it turn around and around before coming to a stop. His curiosity is aroused. He observes the plastic bottle for a time. He leaves it and moves away. Immediately he returns to it. Is the bottle still there, or has it disappeared? He repeats the sequence a number of times, rolls the bottle, and then takes it again in his hands to see if all these interactions have altered it in any way. Altogether he spends about twenty minutes with the bottle, his mind totally concentrated and absorbed by experimentation. I have accompanied him in this exercise, decided only to concentrate and to observe. At first I was feeling irritated and scattered. Now I am centered and whole. I had almost forgotten that I could pay attention so naturally and so undividedly.

Living with Emilio and Jonathan is like living with two scientist-philosopher-artists. Their qualities are contagious. They reach me and expand me. They stimulate my mind and pull it in all directions. Their stories and metaphors awaken my imagination. Their tough questions lead me to think again with a virgin mind. My children's curiosity activates my own by resonance. Their minds, as they create clear, strong ideas, animate my thinking.

I regard my mind as a source of life-giving interest and nourishment. Because I am a writer, a teacher, and a therapist, I also look upon it as a professional tool. I want it to be a well-functioning instrument. I know it needs maintenance, and I believe I can always find new ways of fine-tuning and using it. Being with my children has helped me to develop a few golden rules in using my mind:

Admit the possibility of being mistaken. Since I have become a father, all my beliefs, from ideas on education to the best way of cutting toast, have been challenged. I have sometimes found these challenges refreshing, sometimes exhausting, always useful. Letting my certainties be eroded rather than holding on to them has given me a good measure of healthy skepticism and intellectual vulnerability.

Be a beginner again. Start anew. Go back to the essence. Can I explain it—an event, an idea, a machine—to a child? If not, I do not really understand its meaning myself. Why does a mirror show the world left to right but not upside down? asks Emilio. Well, I don't know. In writing a letter or preparing a lecture, I find myself asking simple questions, taking a fresh look at old beliefs, and valuing the art of simplicity.

Encourage curiosity. That is how, after all, the human race has survived. Curiosity is one of our greatest assets. If a new interest or question arises in my mind, I will not regard it as a waste of time or just ignore it, as I would sometimes do in the past. Instead, I welcome it and let it develop. It is exciting to be curious again.

Value symbols and metaphors. "I am like a boat on a stormy sea," "I feel imprisoned," "This is a trap," "I feel a new wave of vitality," "You are my treasure." We use symbols all the time, mostly without even knowing it. Nowadays I find myself rediscovering this way of thinking. I find that it gives greater depth of meaning. If I want to understand a situation better, I ask myself, what metaphor would a poet—or a child—adopt in this case?

Leave space for the nonrational. Logic and reason are okay, but is that all? Being with children has shown me that we have forms of intelligence that run deeper than $2 + 2 = 4$ or $E = mc^2$. "I know something but I cannot give any logical proof," "I feel it in my bones." Yes, I want to listen more to my intuition and my instinct.

Concentrate on what interests me. I am sure we have taught children how not to pay attention. The culture of the remote control, superficially moving from one subject to another, has influenced the way we think and relate. Can we let children teach us how to pay attention? As for myself, I am getting back in touch with the joy of being concentrated on a subject—nature, music, ideas—that interests me passionately. I throw away the remote control and plunge into my interest. Body and soul. Like a child.

Finally, there is another effect of a different order that being around my children stimulates in my thinking. Emilio and I are returning home one night in the car. He is in the back in his car seat. We have been talking for a while, and now he is silent. It is late. Has he fallen asleep? No. After a long silence, he says, "Daddy, tomorrow let's look up the encyclopedia to see what 'soul' means." What has been going on in his mind? Why is he suddenly talking about this subject? I would like to ask but feel it would be intruding. I try to guess what he is thinking and simply reply, "Okay." We go back to the silence of the night. Emilio, satisfied, is falling asleep. It is a beautiful night in May, the stars are shining. The human mind is a mystery, and I am filled with wonder.

My mind is stimulated not only by way of resonance, however. There is another, more laborious, but equally fertile way it can be switched on. Every day, life with my children offers choices, challenges, problems, and difficulties. My mind, like that of any other parent, is required to develop readiness of spirit, intelligence of the heart, inventiveness. Sometimes I react bluntly and awkwardly. I just follow my conditioning. At other times I do better.

My day-to-day life provides some examples. We are in the car, about to leave a parking lot. Someone has seen us and is waiting for our parking place. Behind him, other cars are waiting to drive through. Suddenly Emilio says he wants to play with the gear stick and brakes. "Emilio, now is not the time to play," I tell him. I cannot bear to keep people waiting. Someone honks, and I become even more agitated. Emilio insists. I pick him up, strap him in the car seat, and we go. Emilio bursts out crying. Maybe I did the only thing I could do. Still, I did not show readiness of spirit, no inventiveness. For me, it is a small defeat.

On another occasion, Emilio starts to be difficult. He does not want the scrambled egg I have just prepared for him but insists on a soft-boiled one. He is being a small tyrant. I can simply say scrambled or nothing, but I see that he is tired, frustrated, cranky; for that matter, so am I. Furthermore, I do not like wasting an egg. I also hate to be mistreated and bossed around by my son, or to end the day on a sour note. I am tempted to preach. Instead, I invent a story: There was once a child who always wanted something other than what was given him and whined because nothing was ever good enough. Various people tried in vain to dissuade him from acting this way, till one day a blue elf appeared and said, "Go ahead. Ask for anything you want!" The child asked for so many things that finally he was exhausted and fell asleep. The next day, when he woke up, he was happy and pleased with everything. Emilio is amused and interested. At the end of the story he asks to eat the scrambled egg.

In this instance, rather than engaging in a battle of wills, like two steers with their horns locked in a fight, I find a solution that leaves both dignities intact and satisfies the two parties. We both feel better. We have made one step forward.

Another example. Again, it is evening, the hour of family disintegration. Jonathan has a cold and is irritable. He is crying, wants to be carried about and bounced. When he is with Mother, he wants Father; when he is with Father, he wants Mother. And if we are both with him, he screams even more. He is beside himself. I pick him up, rock him; nothing works. Suddenly I think of something new. I talk with him about all the people who love him and, rapt with interest, he stops crying. I remind him of his favorite activities: looking at the pictures of peas and strawberries in a book, picking little yellow flowers, eating crackers, singing "Happy Birthday." Jonathan pays close attention, and when I stop, he nervously grunts, "Eh!" for me to go on. My mind searches for other ideas. I recall the few words that he knows and likes to say, like "there," when he wants to point to something, and his latest acquisition: "ciao." He likes this one a lot, and pronounces it with great delight: "Taooooo!," as if greeting someone he has not seen for ages. He smiles a big smile. I have made it. I have succeeded in calming him. I take him back to Vivien, whom he greets with a lovely "Taooooo!" Now he is ready to go to sleep. I may not be a genius, but I have handled an emergency and resolved a problem. I feel great.

Every day, every evening, being with my children presents me with a difficulty to resolve, some pain to heal, a confusion to clarify. Parenthood is never a matter of ordinary administration. I cannot get away with it as easily as that. It is an enterprise that calls up all my resources. Each time I fail to solve a problem, to ease a suffering, or to widen a perspective, I feel a sense of guilt, of failure. But when I achieve success, however small, when I evoke my heart, or use my practical imagination, I feel complete and more alive.

Play

One day I decide to photograph Jonathan's smile. A baby's smile is so pure and luminous it could melt the hardest of hearts. Together with a starry sky, wildflowers, and certain mountain landscapes, it is one of the most beautiful sights I know.

Armed with my camera, I wait. Nothing simpler, I think to myself. At this age, babies smile very often. But a surprise awaits me. Jonathan looks at me, serious and attentive. Through the viewfinder I see him studying the camera. He is okay, but no smiles.

I put the camera down, and straightaway Jonathan gives me a marvelous smile—an innocent, toothless smile that fills my heart with tenderness. I instantly take up the camera. The smile disappears. Perhaps it is because he cannot see my face behind the camera. I hold the camera in position and my head to one side so he can continue to see me. Still no luck. As soon as I put the camera down, he smiles another big smile. Is he teasing me?

I begin to produce all those silly noises that usually make babies laugh and adults look like fools. It has always worked with Jonathan. But not this time. The serious face persists. I ask Vivien to talk to him—she always gets his best smiles. Again, no success.

I start to feel ridiculous. Here I am behind the camera, trying, with grotesque sounds and gestures, to evoke the most natural event in the world. I am trying to generate a mood in my child, so as to preserve it in a photograph and possess it forever. By doing this, I lose contact with him and cease enjoying our time together. Finally, I understand that I cannot force what is by nature spontaneous.

I decide to wait and accept that Jonathan may not smile. I shoot some pictures of different expressions: surprise, doubt, interest. I discover they are equally beautiful. I relax. Now I no longer wish to make something happen at all costs. I understand that I have to flow with what is happening. Then, when I least expect it, Jonathan smiles, with perfect timing that seems to be telling me, At last you understand! I have stopped wishing he were a certain way and simply enjoy the contact. This time I even manage to photograph the smile.

Play

The difference between spontaneity and planning is analogous to that between the flow of a brook and the route of a train. One streams around stones and plants, within the banks, sometimes slowing, sometimes more impetuous, here and there reflecting patterns of light, never stopping. The other rattles along, from time to time stopping as planned. We may live like one or the other. We can proceed according to the planned itinerary, strenuously trying to make life conform to our needs, or we can adapt to whatever we meet and flow without effort.

One day I find myself with lots of time to spend with Emilio. On such occasions I usually ask him, "What would you like to do today?" and list all the possibilities. If I let him choose in that way, I feel very democratic. The menu, however, is mine. I choose the various options—to ride bikes, paint, read books. I am also defining the way to look at life itself: as a series of items from which to choose and make the day's plan.

A child's mind does not work this way. Thought and action arise spontaneously and unpredictably, moment to moment. Today I decide not to offer anything. I am silent, allowing Emilio to take the initiative. Emilio wastes no time. He moves easily from one activity to another, inventing new games, without worrying about what's next. He is like a juggler who does not think about how to catch the next ball—he just catches it.

By proposing a menu of activities from which to choose, I only succeed in making his world rigid and compartmentalized. Alternatively, I can learn from him. Naturally and harmoniously one experience develops from another while Emilio and I play. We play at postman, doctor, at making compositions out of stones and dried leaves, at writing, jumping, at mixing and cooking ingredients (there is a different story for each mixture), at inventing new words, counting and sticking stickers, preparing food, telephoning to hear the precise time of day, using scissors and Scotch tape, and many other activities unforeseen by my list.

I come to understand what it means to live spontaneously, how much richer and more fertile is this way of being. At first I feel anxious—about wasting time and living in a way that is incoherent and disordered. It's the anxiety of losing control. Afterward, I really do lose control and follow a rhythm not my own. I feel much more relaxed. It is a new feeling, which never quite leaves me. It is like riding a bike: hard to explain how to do it, but at some point you just know.

I suspect this more relaxed rhythm is part of our original way of being. Learning to be spontaneous is not a matter of acquiring a new ability, but of remembering an old emotion. In losing my need to control, I lose the anxiety and the feeling of effort. In fact, maybe one of the reasons children have so much more energy than we do is that they let themselves go into the rhythm of life.

I am changing. I used to look at the unexpected as an unpleasant intrusion that disrupted my plans. Now I see it as a source of learning. I notice this change especially in my work. In being with people as a therapist, I used to hold in my mind a vision of where my client was headed. Even though I tried to be flexible, I often resented whatever novelties in the client's life distracted us from the journey. Now I see sessions more as adventures. I do not know what is going to happen beforehand. What are we going to learn today? Nothing that is truly new can be planned. I approach a session with fewer expectations and greater curiosity.

Between my old and my new attitude there is a deep difference, which has to do with the very nature of learning and discovery. It is the difference between a tourist, who visits places in the brochure, and the explorer, who has no idea what she is going to find on her journey. One is in control, but meets only what he already knows. The other is more vulnerable, but makes true discoveries.

I notice my way of teaching groups also changes. I used to feel more secure when I mainly lectured. If I had a few important points to make, I was in control, and I would give people a run for their money. If on the other hand, I did not really know what was going to happen and had no set agenda, I felt like an amateur. That was my old way of thinking. Now I realize that you cannot plan true learning—it comes when it wants. So my work with groups is now based on the participants' moment-to-moment experiences, which I have no way of knowing beforehand. The work is to make sense of it. We see learning as it happens. Easy and simple. This is spontaneity.

Sometimes I wake up in the morning, and I do not know what is going to happen that day. It used to be an uncommon occurrence for me. Now that I have children, it is much more frequent. I used to find it intolerable—what a waste of time! What chaos! Now I know that the reality out there waiting to be discovered is infinitely richer than my own plans. My agenda, however imaginative it may be, cannot contain the whole wide unpredictable world.

Spontaneity is an extraordinary gift, and every time we encounter it we feel regenerated. Why is it that a mediocre actor, awkward and false, bores us, while a great actor arouses our enthusiasm? Why does a beginner pianist, laboriously picking out the notes, disturb us, while a great pianist carries us to a world of harmony and happiness? It is because the great actor and the great pianist have attained—after a great deal of work—the very source of spontaneity.

Spontaneity requires an organic trust—a faith that

what happens at any moment is just right. For children, this is not a conscious, reasoned trust, but it is inherent in their way of being. This point becomes clearer to me one day when I watch Jonathan as he wakes up. He takes a toy that was placed next to him during his nap. He grasps it without hesitation or reflection, or even the need to look at it. It is a quick and natural gesture, as when we switch off the light. And yet Jonathan does not know the toy is there. Why does he turn to it as if he were expecting to find it? Why does he grasp the toy? Because it is there.

It seems to me that children, especially very young ones, often have no preferences. When we adults have a program, priorities loom large and ponderous: A is better than B, B is better than C. Fantasies also abound: We imagine what we would like to attain and where we have to go. With fantasies, desires emerge. We are not neutral to the outcome. And desires always come hand in hand with fear—if we do not get what we want, we fail.

Very young children don't function like this. Everything is vital and interesting to them. They have no rigid preferences, but participate in what is, totally and happily. I realize this during our disastrous holiday in the tropics. Having carefully planned our trip, we now find ourselves in a tourist ghetto, a machine scientifically organized to squeeze every cent out of its victims.

Instead of glorious beaches, we find swamps; it rains ceaselessly with gusts of cold wind; the shops sell horrid souvenirs; and the animals, supposedly a star attraction, are maltreated, few, and miserable. A disaster. We feel we have thrown our money away. Nothing goes according to plan, nor according to the tourist brochures. Yet the children have a good time, making do with very little. In our hotel room Emilio learns to do sums, plays ball, draws elevators, plays rough-and-tumble with me, invents game after game. Jonathan smiles at everything and is content if he can practice standing up, crumple paper, or crawl.

Why is it that the children have fun while we parents are unhappy? Because they are more flexible. They had no fantasies to actualize in the first place. They had no expectations. Life is still rich and interesting when it doesn't match our plans—maybe even richer than in the tourist brochure.

A mind without preferences is also a mind without prejudices—ready to learn in any situation, from any person. Here we are, Emilio and I, at Milan station, with two hours to wait between trains. What are we going to do? This place hasn't much to offer a child, or so I think. We go to the wax museum—an underground area, deserted and ignored by travelers. It is populated by famous people of all time, gathered in a kind of grotesque celebration: Pope John, Gorbachev, Marilyn

Monroe, Napoleon, Dante, Garibaldi, Landru, and a couple of soccer stars, all immobile in a transcendental time outside human affairs, and so unreal as to give you goose bumps.

Emilio, however, is passionately interested. He asks me details about the life of each figure, especially Landru. How come he didn't get along with his wives? How could he manage to burn them against their will? Would I do that to Mummy? And who is Dante? Why can he visit hell and we can't? Is he a friend of the soccer stars? We take a tour of the wax works, one by one, then start from the beginning again. Initially, I find the museum banal and in bad taste, but Emilio sees this place as an enchanted castle. By the end, the whole gallery acquires a certain intrigue for me, too, because I have put aside my expectations and see it anew. I am living in the present, unconcerned about what should have happened. I am caught up in the wonder of a child who turns every event into learning material.

Our purpose in going to the wax museum was not to learn something. That happened by chance. I would have preferred to find a park near the station, with trees and a playground for Emilio to have fun with other children. That wasn't available, and those two hours had seemed to me a waste of time. But for a child there is no wasted time. All time is in the present, and it is interesting. The whole world is a playground. Life is not going to happen in two hours from now—it is happening now.

In this occasion I also see the danger of transforming spontaneity into compulsion. We learn by being spontaneous. Our whole being is ready and willing to do so. If, however, we get the idea that we *have* to learn, all becomes artificial—an effortless experience becomes analyzed and taught. It is like teaching someone how to be hungry, or how to be in love, or how to have an orgasm. Whatever is touched by this perversion will never again be spontaneous.

So it is with children. It is exhausting to think of what they have to learn before they can move about competently in the world. The task is enormous: learning to walk, to talk, to tie shoelaces, twirl spaghetti on the fork, behave in public, wait their turn, understand time and space, read and write, and so on. Yet all this happens without much effort—if there are no interferences. Emilio, three years old, phones me at work to wish me happy birthday. I find out later that he did it all by himself. How did he learn to dial my number? No one taught him. He has only seen his mother do it. He has absorbed this procedure as easily as he sleeps or breathes.

Maybe we are trying to teach too many things to children, rather than learning what they may have to teach us. One day Emilio is rude to Vivien. I feel he should say sorry, but instead I explain that Mummy is sad because of it. I hope that before he goes to sleep he can make up with her in some way. There is not a word about this matter for three hours. Finally, while he is sitting on the potty, Emilio asks his mummy to sing him a song. It is a melancholy, melodious song she had not sung to him for a long time—since those magical days when he was a one-year-old. That is his way of making peace, of saying, Let's love each other like we did in those times. It is a much more touching and original way to say "I am sorry" than the bureaucratic style I had in mind. I am glad he did not learn what I wanted to teach him.

Slowly but surely I am cultivating a more receptive attitude. I intervene less, I observe, sometimes I look on in wonder. It is an attitude we have to a large extent lost in our day. The tendency is to be more active: to break, tear, change, direct, tame, exploit. But if we adopt a certain kind of respect, of waiting, we can see much more. We often desperately want to act instead of not to act, to talk instead of remaining silent, to reach conclusions rather than accept uncertainty, to show we are right rather than listen, to possess instead of enjoying. These are universal tendencies, at least in our culture, even in the most passive and apathetic individuals.

To listen. To be. To let it happen. These are meditative attitudes we have forgotten—and yet they could help us all rediscover love and wonder.

One morning I lie down next to Emilio just as he is waking up. I like to see him gradually coming to full consciousness and beginning to think. I am tempted to ask him how he is, how he slept, what he dreamed, the usual questions parents ask their kids. Instead I wait. Emilio is awake. He looks at the ceiling, his eyes darting rapidly. From the rhythm of his breathing I know that he is reflecting. I am bursting to ask him what he is thinking about, but I know he would only answer in the way all children respond to this kind of intrusion: Nothing. I would only be interrupting the flow of his thoughts. I manage to control myself and remain in silence with him. My mind becomes still. A full hour goes by. I feel Emilio continuing to think. Finally he says, "Daddy, what is the difference between 'perhaps' and 'maybe'?"

What were Emilio's thoughts in that hour? I will never know, nor would I have known had I asked. That's the way the cookie crumbles. Meanwhile, I had learned an important lesson in the art of silence.

The most exquisite form of spontaneity is play. True, play often contains rules, but its essence is other than the rules. It is a quality of freedom, of effortless pleasure and vitality. Watch puppies play: They delight us because they are so fresh and they have so much fun. It is the same with children. If we enter their world, we will connect with the spirit of play—a special wavelength of the mind that elevates and liberates us. Human beings toil and struggle. Play is a privilege of the gods, but of children, too. Playing with my children, I have found this thrill that frees the mind of heaviness and worry.

It is not always a complete success. Often children's games are boring and repetitive. Emilio likes to play the "trading game": He groups all his little toys and collection of objects, such as stones, gems, toy cars, key holders, little balls, and so on, divides them into two groups, keeps one, and leaves you the other. Then the trading starts. I will give you this if you give me that, and so forth. For some reason, Emilio feels the need to go on for hours, and it can get quite boring. I do it with him out of goodwill and fatherly duty. In our family, it has become a legend: Who is going to play the "trading game" today? Yes, playfulness is a state of grace, and it is not always available, or perhaps it is always available to children, just not for adults.

Take the first time I play soccer with Emilio, however. This is different. Soccer was my passion. I bounce the ball, hit it with the head then with the foot again, stop it, keep it moving on the grass, challenge Emilio to take it away from me, and make it disappear behind him. I am showing off. He is impressed, and I enjoy that, too. At first I prevail over Emilio, of course, because he is a beginner. Then I let him take the upper hand, but he wants me to play for real, or at least, he decides, at seventy percent of my ability. What fun! When was the last time I played soccer? Twenty years ago, maybe, but the fun is still wired into me, waiting to explode.

Jonathan and I play at constructing with wooden blocks. We each make a building, and he has very good taste and sense of proportion. Then I become engrossed in my own building. You should see what a marvel I build. I am completely taken by the excitement of creation and forget everything else. This is as absorbing as a dream. In the end I find myself thinking that I should have been an architect—and woe betide anyone who knocks it down!

Another time I play hide-and-seek with both my children. They have to look for me. I think of less obvious places, such as inside a cupboard or a bed. Yes, under a bed. Then I wait. I can hear them coming, they are excited and a little scared, too, because some rooms are dark. Dad is nowhere to be found—did he go away? If I feel they are becoming anxious, I make some funny sound, so they know I am around, but they still cannot find me. I have a great time as I keep them wondering. In the end they find me and we all laugh together. And sometimes—the very best times— I ask myself, Why am I not doing this all the time? I believe that when we ask ourselves that question, that is a very good sign. We probably *should* be doing that all the time.

Jokes are part of playing as well. They have a degree of mischievousness, which, when it is not offensive, is a great way to transform our aggression. Jonathan puts the mask of the Big Bad Wolf on my bed, right on the cushion, pretending the Wolf is sleeping there. Then he waits behind the door to see my reaction. I pretend I am scared. He is very amused. Therefore I am very amused. Another time we are invited to the seventieth birthday party of a man we know. He starts giving a solemn talk about aging and what a great achievement it is to reach seventy. He thinks age has made him wise. Before him stands a big chocolate cake. Emilio eyes it for a while, then interrupts the speech: "You are not keeping all that cake for yourself, are you?" Everybody is amused, except the seventy-year-old man. The interruption was rude, but I admit I find it hard not to burst out laughing. Also, I realize how solemn we all are, we grown-ups, how much we take ourselves seriously instead of realizing that life is just a game.

Experimenting is also great fun. We like to do scientific experiments. For instance, let us make a volcano. We go outside, dig some wet sand, put a can with bicarbonate of soda in it and red color, mold the sand all around it like a volcano, then pour in some vinegar. Out comes a red explosion of lava. I watch the children's faces. They are fascinated and thrilled, and I am, too.

I enjoy experimenting, and I enjoy joking, and I love playing. I find all that fun in myself again. Yes, this is one of the greatest blessings in life—to lighten up, to become again, for a short while, a child at play.

Innocence

Destination: play park, three blocks away. Emilio has discovered the tricycle. He pedals happily while I walk behind.

But reaching the playground takes us two hours. Our short walk becomes an adventure in a foreign land. We start with the no parking sign. Emilio wants to understand that mysterious red and blue circle with the oblique line, and why cars are not allowed here, and whether or not we can stop there, and who put up the sign, and what happens if a car does stop there, and who will come out of the driveway, and so on. Next we meet the little red man and the little green man at the traffic lights. What fun to watch them appear and to shout, "Now!" when they change into one another!

A billboard shows a child with a mouth in the shape

of a triangle, eating a triangle biscuit. That fascinates Emilio. Out of a crack in the sidewalk grows a tiny flower worthy of attention. And how can we ignore the dog shit in the form of a six?

At first I am impatient. Weren't we heading to the play park? Well, then, go ahead and pedal, and stop wasting time. Let us stick to our plan. Soon, however, I realize that this short trip is a grand journey. It is not a boring urban road from A to B, but a microcosm.

Take the telephone booth, for instance. What do you insert in the slot? A phone card. Well, let's do it. We experiment with various calls, the numbers appearing and disappearing on the small LCD screen, strange sounds, the recorded voice that tells the time, the card that comes out again after you hang up, imaginary conversations with Mummy, with the doctor, with Grandfather, attempts at inserting a pine needle into the slot, et cetera. And what about the Alfa Romeo sign with the snake? What is a snake doing up there? Suddenly everything looks puzzling, perhaps magical, to me, too. The journey continues. We look at people's names on the doorbells: Press the button and you hear someone's voice. And the round brass doorknob reflects the whole world.

I understand that a young child experiences time in a different way than we adults do. For us time is like an arrow, pointing in one direction. We have to reach a goal—all else is secondary. Ours is an efficient but impoverished time. Children's time, instead, is like a circle. It doesn't go anywhere. It is inefficient. They would miss every train, in fact there would be no train timetable at all if we functioned that way. But this is an open time, in which anything can happen and everything is a surprise. It is all new and interesting. In this state everything we meet is gratuitous. Here we enjoy the absolute freshness of experience. This is innocence.

At first I am annoyed for having to trade in my familiar way of being for this less structured outlook. But gradually I see that the means is as important as the end, in fact that the means and the end are the same thing. I feel the knot in my solar plexus dissolving, a knot I had been living with for who knows how long. It is possible to live in the here and now, free-floating, without going anywhere, because wherever we find ourselves we have already arrived.

All I need to do to understand what this attitude entails is to go over the events of a day with Emilio, an exercise he likes a lot. While for us grown-ups a day is often just another day, for a child a day is an intellectual saga. Today we went to the bank and the post office; then you had a tantrum because you wanted to eat the toothpaste; you built a house with the sofa pillows; you went for a walk and picked flowers, found snail shells and a heart-shaped pebble; you typed your name with the computer; you drew angry faces; you played shop; you stuck pencils into the VCR; you put your peas in the dessert and then you ate it. . . .

It is a useful exercise for me, too, because then I see why any one day is unique. My days, more or less like each other, are anonymous and are over so quickly. To my child, each day is an epic, it lasts a century.

Children are innocent; what we perceive according to our assumptions, they see in a new and open way. This happens in just about every aspect of life. Take competitiveness, for instance—the premise that so frequently colors our feelings and relations. A friend told me his son had won a race and had been awarded a trophy. During the prize-giving, just after receiving his award, he turned to his friends to reassure them: "Don't worry, you will get one, too." For him the trophy did not mean he had prevailed over his friends. It was a present every participant got for having played. Day after day we try to instill in the minds of our children the competitive, play-to-win attitude—and in the end we succeed. Perhaps we should let them influence us in a view of the world where everybody wins, has fun, and wants the others' happiness as much as his own.

I try to imagine how Emilio, not yet one year old, sees the world, at an age when he does not have words for expressing himself. Judging by his interest and expressions, it is a surprising world: The leaves moving on the branches of a tree outline waves of pure energy, the reflections on a metal object are an otherworldly effulgence, the intricate drawings on a book cover are a labyrinth, a tulip is a colored abyss into which you can plunge.

The fact that young children probably see a purer version of the world than we do has many repercussions. I remember when my godson Jason, at ten months, saw an ant for the first time—one quite large and impressive. For a few moments I also saw that ant for the first time. What a strange sight. We take ants for granted, but when you see one for the first time and you have no categories in which to place it, it is indeed an amazing event—no less than a dinosaur or a unicorn walking down the street would be for us adults. A continual unfolding of ever-new forms, visions devoid of any previous reasoning or memory or preference, in the pure state: This is how a child sees reality.

I had a similar experience when, together with Jason, I saw a musical band. What does it look like to a child when a band, with trombones and drums, suddenly appears in the street and produces music? A numinous display of gleaming brass and red uniforms, of strong sounds and proud marching. When I am with a child, I participate in his amazement.

I realize a child's clear perception is contagious. I

understand that living in my own clichés is to perceiving the world anew what canned produce is to fresh food. The key is the quality of experience. My experience can be tired, worn out, empty: Because I have had it so many times, I am not really interested in having it again. It becomes a gray, dusty code in my mind. Or I can start from scratch, like a child. A face, a flower, a piece of music, a feeling, an idea—anything can be new again. And then it becomes a source of wonder. I simply ask myself, how would my child look at it?

Jonathan watches a cement mixer turning and making a cavernous rumbling sound. He looks inside and sees a black circle. It is a dark and frightening precipice; no, it is a vortex turning and trying to pull you inside. All at once the cement mixer no longer looks to me like an ordinary part of the urban scenery. It is a preternatural entity, commanding terror and awe. As I hold Jonathan, I can feel that he is attracted and at the same time cautious. He does not want to go too close. What an extraordinary apparition!

Around nine months, Jonathan discovers water. He is fascinated by the liquid that runs out of the tap or the sponge. Is it solid? What is this strange phenomenon you can put your fingers through? When you touch it, it gives you a pleasant feeling, and you can splash and spray it all over the place. What on earth is it?

Jonathan discovers knees, his own and those of others. Yes, knees. There is something fascinating about legs bending and stretching. Or again, a plastic bag flying about in a piazza, blown by the wind on a sunny Sunday afternoon: What a surrealistic sight. Distant sounds are another discovery. You simply have to stop and listen to an airplane in the distance, a bulldozer, the wind, thunder, someone opening a creaking door in the next room. Jonathan's eyes reveal keen attention. Each sound I take for granted is to him a secret code to unravel.

It occurs to me that a child still lives outside the culture into which she is born. She also lives, for the time being, outside of history. She will gradually enter, and she will be guided in by us. But at first she is outside, and therefore her viewpoint is still as pure as can be. Sometimes it is the child who takes us into her world, and for some moments we, too, can be outside history.

For me it is like glimpsing a long-hidden treasure. As a child, I, too, was innocent. Later, like everyone, I lost my innocence and fell into the all too human world of compromises and calculations, of habits and stereotypes. Everything took on a grayish tint. Now, alongside my kids, I am readmitted, for a few moments now and then, into the room of treasures. Here I can once again be amazed, here life is timeless, guilt and shame are unknown, all is scintillating and new. I now have the chance to rediscover the ineffable.

To let go of the end-oriented way of seeing the

world can be difficult and uncomfortable. Try driving for an hour to take your child to the zoo, only to find that he does not look dutifully at lions, monkeys, and giraffes, but instead chases the pigeons. "Emilio, look at that lovely koala!" No, just ordinary old pigeons. But for Emilio they are not commonplace, because nothing is commonplace to a child.

Too often we adults live in the realm of "been there, done that," a rather sad and narrow realm. Wherever we look, we find something we already know and therefore we think we do not have to examine it any further. We are living in a film we have already seen. Our only pleasure consists in showing the film to someone who has not yet seen it. But for children the world shines with the novelty and the intensity of the first viewing, like the first kiss, the first day at school, the first rainbow.

One day, following the instructions in a book on elementary geometry, I am cutting colored cardboard shapes: triangle, square, circle, in red, blue, yellow, and green. I have been to the stationery shop for the very purpose of buying colored cardboard and have taken a lot of time to cut out the shapes precisely. The aim is to teach Emilio set theory and geometric classification. There are lots of educational games you can play with the various shapes.

When Emilio sees the colored shapes, he is immediately fascinated. For a second I think I am on the right track: The subject is interesting. I will be able to teach him what I want. A few million brain cells are about to go into action.

Well, are they? Perhaps—but not the ones I had in mind. Ignoring my suggestions, Emilio makes up a long story out of the bits of cardboard, then asks me for some Scotch tape so he can stick them onto a page and make a collage, and finally he wants to mail them to a girlfriend as a gift. He has distorted the rules of the game. This time I do not feel frustrated and resist the temptation to press on with my teaching, which, if I think about it, is actually quite boring. Emilio's ideas are much more brilliant.

For a child, every act, every attitude, and every object is, it seems to me, just itself and nothing more. This kind of perception is precise and clear-cut. We grown-ups, instead, look at the world through the filter of our associations and memories, which inflate and deform what we see. Think of how many connotations sexuality has for us: fear and apprehension, desire and repression, memories and fantasies. One word is enough to evoke an enormous baggage of associations. One day Emilio is mistaken for a girl, an error that often occurs because of his long hair. But he promptly pulls his pants down and says, "No, I am a boy. Look at my penis!"

What would the sexual act be like for us in this state of mind? We could learn a lot from such innocence, were we not already conditioned with our embarrassment, our fears, and our giggling, to communicate repression. In the shop where this scene takes place, heads turn, and I smile, embarrassed. People are amused, but also slightly uncomfortable, as often happens when someone tells it like it is.

Innocence is a state free of structures. There are none of the knobs and handles to which we are accustomed. Consider this episode. I am making myself a coffee as usual. Jonathan in the next room, with characteristic timing, interrupts my ritual: "Daaaaaaaaddy!" "Yes?" I ask, a little annoyed. Silence. A moment later, "Nothing." I may be wrong, but I think I detected a touch of amusement in his voice. Soon enough, he starts again: "Daaaaaaaaaaaddy!" "Yes, what is it?" If he is calling me, he must want something, or need help. Perhaps he must want me to play with him. Or has he hurt himself? Silence. Then, "Nothing." The third time, I finally get it. He simply likes calling me, hearing my voice, he in one room, I in another. I join him in his game: "Jonathaaaaaaan." "What?" This time I am silent for a few moments, then I say, "Nothing." I hear Jonathan laughing. We are having fun. I have rid myself of my mental schemas and for the moment am a little more innocent.

Innocence

Emilio and Jonathan, for the time being, are living in innocence. I can learn to rediscover my own innocence. I manage to free myself at times of my ideas and calculations. I realize this is the same territory trodden by those who meditate or pray. I try to be receptive instead of leading my children at all costs to buy my assumptions. I let them take me by the hand and show me a world sparkling with wonder.

Will

I am at the top of a strange slippery dip. Who on earth invented this contraption? It is made of rollers that turn when you slide down, and it is quite high. From below it looks harmless, but not so from above. Now I know why a child sometimes hesitates before going down. I feel dizzy. Why did I have to climb up? Because Emilio asked, of course. He gave me no peace till I agreed.

"Come on, Daddy, you, too!"

"No, slippery dips are only for children."

"But there aren't any other children."

"I am too big."

"But look, the slippery dip is big, too—you will fit."

"You have to learn to play by yourself."

"Yes, but I like to play with you, too."

Emilio, however, is not as insistent as usual. I know I could get away with a refusal. He would play on his own. But that doesn't feel right. Deep down, I want to have fun with him. On the other hand, it would be easier to sit on a bench and just watch. Will I or won't I? I decide to go.

I feel awkward. I fight my own laziness. I let myself go. The slippery dip is fast. The rollers massage my body. Emilio is happy. Going down, I feel shaken and abused. In a whirlwind of sensations, I think that this descent symbolizes perfectly a parent's life: forbidden to sit quietly, you lose control. You are pushed around. It is all rather uncomfortable. You wonder how you ever got into this. Fun is a lot of work. And you are massaged on all sides.

Going down the slippery dip was an act of will. I decided to do it, to participate, even if the line of least resistance would have been to avoid the ordeal. During the three-second descent, I understand how easy it would be to cop out and sit on the sidelines. I see how my children—if I allow them—can shake me out of my lethargy. I see that in my life as a parent I can activate that precious capacity—the will—which increases my inner strength.

In the slippery dip episode, I had to decide to play instead of to sit on the bench. At other times I simply have to decide to be present. At any moment with my kids the question arises: How much of myself am I willing to give? The only answer that works is: One hundred percent. With children you cannot be available part time.

I am giving Jonathan his breakfast. He likes to have a variety of foods to nibble: sultanas, a piece of bread, banana, apple. I have prepared them, and, believing myself free to take ten minutes off, I glance at the book I am reading. I do not read even half a page, and Jonathan sounds out, "Uh, uh." He cannot talk yet, but communicates very well. Food is not enough; he wants my company—not my halfhearted presence. He wants me. I, however, want to go on reading. After giving him a word or two to keep him happy, I try again. A few seconds go by, and he utters his "Uh, uh," this time reaching out his hand to touch me. I don't give up, but add a biscuit to his plate, one of those hard, crunchy ones he has to suck on. This one is worth a good ten minutes' attention. I resume reading. Once again his voice sounds more insistent: "Uh! Uh!"

I realize I cannot read and that anyway I want to be with this baby. It is the right thing. We look into each other's eyes. Although he obliged me, it was nevertheless an act of will on my part to turn my attention to him. In deciding to be there, I feel whole, completely here, and know it is right.

I discover this sense of integrity in another way,

too—in keeping my promises at all costs. We should keep our promises to everyone, but children have a particularly strong sense of justice. If betrayed, they are furious. One morning before leaving for work, I tell Jonathan that at night I will put him to bed, a ritual he likes a lot. But I arrive home too late and he is already fast asleep. I ask Vivien how the evening has been. Did he remember my promise? No, it seems. He was a little angel. The next morning while I am in the bathroom shaving, Jonathan opens the door, frowning and indignant. His look, without words, tells me everything. I had let him down. Knowing I would be late, I should have called to tell him. Once again I realize the importance of integrity. I want to keep my promises and make the effort to be consistent, rather than forgetting about it and hoping everything will be okay. For this purpose I need will.

Emilio and I are on the street. We see a child coming out of a shop with an enormous turquoise ice cream covered with little candy balls. "Buy me one of those!" The fascination of the turquoise, his favorite color, and the ice cream, his favorite food, is an irresistible combination. But I am firm. It will soon be dinnertime, and besides, Emilio has already had an ice cream today. I say no. He becomes enraged. He screams, throws himself onto the ground, punches me, cries desperately—everything he can do to embarrass me in public. Heads turn. He shrieks, "One ice cream, pleeeeeeeeeeeaaase, I am only asking for an ice cream!"

The temptation to give in is strong. Emilio would be satisfied and happy, and I would get out of this unpleasant situation. In the past I have yielded many times, and Emilio has perfected his awful techniques of persuasion. I have often proclaimed a rule and soon afterward contradicted it. "Oh, why not make an exception?" After all, an ice cream is not the end of the world. Why be stubborn about it? This temper tantrum will spoil the family's evening.

But no. I know it is not right, and I must honor my own words. Calmly and firmly, I say no to all his pleading performances. In the past, when I have given in, despite the immediate rewards of tranquillity, I have felt like an amoeba. Emilio himself has noted my inconsistency: "You always give in anyway." Or else, when I would threaten punishment: "You always talk about it and never do it." There was a weakness, a surrendering, a falseness in all this. I had belied the power of my word. The kindness of my yes was the false kindness of someone retreating. My words had no more value. I had lost face.

A simple no now shows me resoluteness. It is a useful word. When you are a parent, you have to know how to say it often, and well—without anger, pride, or guilt. A simple, pure no. This, too, is my will.

"No" is an uncomfortable word. It causes conflict, rebellion, sulking. "Yes" is a much nicer choice. It costs nothing at first and brings enthusiasm, gratitude, euphoria. But if I say yes all the time, my yes loses its meaning. No is needed, too. It restores integrity and credibility. Yes may be a landslide. No is a bulwark.

The will is essential. My work as psychotherapist has shown me its importance. Those who have not found it, or have lost it, are depressed and disoriented. I rediscover it with my kids. I have often felt that I am at their mercy, that they have deprived me of my will. Many parents feel this way, especially the more permissive ones like me. With great effort and difficulty I have seen that sometimes I have to be unpopular. It is better for the children, and for me, too. I know who I am, no longer an amoeba, but a human being who takes a stand.

A parent's life is a mine of possibilities for pretending, forgetting, cheating, and wiggling out of difficult situations. Take holding back, for instance. With our children it is common because they require so much work. I have chosen to give them my best, yet often I cheat. I know that reading a story or chatting with Emilio at bedtime is good for him. But maybe I am tired and I pretend I have forgotten. If instead I make the effort, I end up feeling better, and so does he. We have rounded off the day instead of giving in to fatigue and disintegration.

I have just washed Jonathan and changed his clothes. But now he decides that he wants to go back and play with the mud. It would be very comfortable to distract him, but is it right? It is great fun for a child getting his hands in the earth, getting dirty and messing around freely. All right: back to the mud.

Will, by itself, makes me neither stricter nor more indulgent. It simply enables me to affirm with clarity what I choose. We are at a restaurant and we hear a baby crying. Jonathan is alarmed and wants to go and find out why, perhaps console the baby. I know this is important for him, and I like the idea of encouraging his empathy. But I am lazy and fear making a fool of myself. Worse still, the pasta will get cold. We go nevertheless. This, too, is will.

Emilio has his bit of pocket money, but it is not enough for the stickers he wants to buy. He demands that I make up the difference. I am tempted to give him a few coins. However, which is the better way for learning the value of money? I decide not to give him the extra money. He can wait for his next pay, calculate, learn that money does not come easily, accept his own financial limits. Another unpopular decision, bringing whining and argument. Yet I know I have done the right thing.

This is not perfectionism. I know that in bringing up children you often have to compromise, content yourself, and let be. But whatever you do in life, you can do well or amateurishly, your mind elsewhere. I want to do it well.

I am thinking of the work done on a house: tiles laid untidily, bumpy plaster, a sink badly installed, an electrical circuit made in a hurry. Then and there you don't notice, but over time you understand the difference—and so does the tradesman himself. A builder once did a job for me—very poor quality. When I pointed it out to him, he apologized, saying: "*A ogni poeta gli manca un verso*. Every poet misses a verse." Maybe he thought he was funny, yet I doubt he went away satisfied. The man who painted the exterior of our house was very different: He did a fine job and respected even the swallows' nests just under the roof line. He was a man proud of his work, content with himself. Competence, precision, dedication—perhaps they take effort, but they fulfill us.

So, too, with children. Bringing them up is our creation, and it can be a job well or sloppily done. "God is in the details." Many can perform well on the grand occasions, but you see a person's real value in how she handles the small tasks.

Finally, there is another area where I can find my will: in reclaiming my own world of interests and activities. One night I dream that my precious camera, of which I am extremely fond, is covered in sticky apple juice concentrate, which has entered inside the very mechanism, ruining it beyond repair. Horrified, I wake up and straightaway understand the significance of the dream. The camera is my creative world and my connection to beauty; the apple juice, which we use as a sweetener, represents my kids. The two little rascals have invaded my space, messed around with a treasured part of my life. Another night I dream I have to play a violin concert on a Stradivarius that, in the dream, belongs to me. The hour of the performance draws near, and I realize I have lost my most precious instrument. I wake up in a panic—am I losing my art, my creativity?

It is all clear to me now. If I do not want to lose myself, I must learn to protect my space. It requires determination. With will and firmness I gain ground, like clearing a space in the jungle. I take more time for myself, do what I like to do. I spend time with Vivien; I read, write, see friends, even take photographs of flowers, which is my passion. As I walk out of the house, I hear Emilio accusing, "You are never here!" But when I come back, I am much happier and more present— and the children are, too. It has not been easy, but I have found myself again.

Sometimes will makes me care more for others. At other times it helps me care for myself. In itself, the will is neutral, an instrument that multiplies my possibilities. The will in itself has no content. A car has no fixed, built-in destination. It allows you to go where you want to go. The more will you have, the more choices are within your reach—choices that, because of habit, inertia, guilt, or fear, you would not have had. The will makes you neither firmer nor more permissive. It allows you to be one way now and another way tomorrow. It makes you neither more available to others nor more self-assertive. It opens up your possibilities. You have a greater repertoire. The choice is yours.

I believe a big source of pain for all of us is being what we do not want to be, doing what we do not want to do. It is the feeling of not being in charge. It leads to depression and discouragement. With my children I discover that I can be present instead of absent. That I can be strong instead of weak. Or flexible when I am habitually rigid. Or diligent when I tend to be sloppy. Or healthily selfish when guilt would have made me a compulsory altruist. The content of my choice is always changing, but the feeling is familiar: I am not pushed around by outer circumstances or inner feelings. I am in charge.

It is like a muscle that slowly develops. At first I am painfully aware that the muscle is not there. In the new situation of being a father, all my weak spots become visible, and I realize how little will I have. To have no choice feels like a prison. Then I develop the muscle, because I use it. I have more choices. I feel more competent. It is a great feeling.

Will. Life with my children offers me a thousand occasions for cultivating it—a will that need not be severe and dictatorial. A will that is loyal to that in which I believe, which makes me courageous, firm, and persistent. It has countless faces, all with one and the same result: They all lead me to a diamondlike energy, with its many cutting edges, yet whole, strong, and luminous.

Love

Four-month-old Jonathan smiles at us. Vivien and I play with him. He is delighted. He simply enjoys being with us. This is happiness. With his little arm movements he says, More, more. It is such fun, he wants to keep it up. Laughing, he seems to be saying, How wonderful to love. It is like a rich banquet—there is plenty for everyone. Yes, this is love, contented love with no inhibitions, a love material and spiritual at the same time. Jonathan is free. He thinks neither about what he has received nor about what he has to give. Gratuitous love, here and now. It is so simple. Why don't we all do the same all the time?

I feel great tenderness. It is a natural reaction. You see it in the animal world. Young mammals have survived by evoking such tenderness. The ones who couldn't do so were eaten by wolves. But this is not just survival strategy. It is pure fun. Like Jonathan, I enjoy myself. His freedom is contagious. All love should be like this—free, without expectations, judgments, or comparisons.

I notice how hard it is to let myself go and let myself love this freely—how risky. First I have to go through some barriers. Danger. Forbidden. No crossing over. Alarm. Then I realize that if I risk entering a world so beautiful, I might forget all else, lose the sense of time, never want to go back. I hesitate a moment. The emotion is too strong.

We have all learned dozens of ways to hide our real feelings. Otherwise we would be too open and vulnerable. Beauty shakes and shocks us—and so transforms us. I decide to risk and let this love in. It is wonderful.

In the blackest moments, life seems senseless—a mechanism full of puffing pistons, gauges, wheels producing nothing. I think of time swallowing everything up and nothing having any value in this precarious existence. Even the great triumphs of humanity—Beethoven's symphonies, Shakespeare's works, the words of Christ, Einstein's theories—will all one day end in nothing.

Parenthood makes this perception fully evident. Day after day I work, run around, get upset, worry. I am cook, waiter, porter, driver, teacher, nurse, babysitter, clown. A big machine turns relentlessly, grinding out fatigue, hours and days, fears and pleasures, words and laughter, cries and screams. What is all that for? Isn't it all senseless? The only certainty left is nothingness.

Then the state of grace descends and saves me. One moment of love changes everything. It is love that bestows sense on what otherwise would be empty and useless, love with its beauty and warmth, making the miracle.

Is there anything that can reawaken our tenderness more than being with a baby? I have seen many people cast aside their frowns while with a child. They become softer, their hearts fill with warmth. This tenderness loosens us when we are tense and brightens us when we are in the dark. It is what makes life worth living. A second of this love is worth years of struggle and disillusion.

And now let us imagine what would happen if we took away all feeling from love—what would be left? A lot. Intelligence, for instance. If I think about how I like to be loved, I imagine that someone understands my most basic needs as well as my dreams and aspirations. It certainly beats hugs and kisses. One day I tell Emilio for the twentieth time that I love him. He replies, "Stop telling me all the time. You can say I love you once a day. Now give me something to eat. I'm hungry." That is what love should be like—no gushing fanfare but a readiness to understand and to help each other through the turbulence of life.

This kind of love means putting yourself in another's shoes, understanding how she feels and what she wants. Emilio wants to binge on sultanas, but he has just had an intestinal infection. He is better off without them. I say no, and he has a tantrum: "I want sultanas!" Suddenly sultanas have assumed a momentous importance, as though his survival—and our relationship—depended on them. I put my foot down. No is no. He, too, hardens. He cries and screams. A battle of wills.

Finally, he looks at me and says, "But can't I have half a sultana?" Surely that won't hurt him. I give it to him and he calms down. Sultanas were not the issue, his pride was. That half a sultana saved face for him, and it gave me an opportunity to understand him.

Jonathan is crying. Why? Does he want cuddling, a clean diaper, does he want to go outside, or to eat? No, he is thirsty. I thought about what he might need and worked it out. My understanding makes not only him feel better, but me as well—not just because he stopped crying, but because each time I understand, something inside me relaxes, and there is more light. Love, I think, is just this practical intelligence, knowing, moment to moment, what others need. Living with children is a continuous exercise, like a quiz with questions of increasing difficulty, that put even the most empathic intelligence to the test.

Caring for another, I forget myself—and that is a marvelous gift. For many years I have been studying the processes of growth, how we can evolve, have better relations with others, free ourselves of our blocks, enjoy beauty. I have concluded that we cannot grow deliberately. It happens by itself, like a flower that opens or a seed that sprouts. However, the right conditions must be there. The space in which we can grow and expand and breathe freely is too often cluttered with our anxieties, our struggles, or the very desire to grow. The more we think about ourselves, the less likely it is that we grow. If instead something worthwhile absorbs our attention—an idea, a value, another person—then we grow without even noticing it. We realize it afterward.

Raising children seems to me the best teaching of self-forgetfulness. Children's demands, so frequent and so clamorous, their rhythms, so pressing, leave little room for thinking about ourselves. We gradually become more disinterested, and act without expecting something in return. I feel great when that happens. If my mind is unconcerned about receiving my due, I feel freer, because I have nothing to gain or to lose. Taking care of my kids engrosses me so much that as long as I do not complain or feel sorry for myself, I really do forget myself.

There is another surprising benefit—gratitude. As all parents, my parents were not perfect, but they both deserve credit for never having flung in my face all that they had done for me—an archetypal temptation when you have children. When I became a father and faced the daily saga of bringing up a child, I would give myself points for all I was doing: how disinterested and self-sacrificing I am, what work, what dedication! Then I realized that someone else had done the same—if not more—for me.

As a child, like all children, I was helpless, needed food and support and care. My parents fed and supported me. At that time I took it for granted. As an adult I was too busy to comprehend it. But as a father, working around the clock, forfeiting my spare time, exhausted at the end of the day, looking ahead to countless similar days, I realized that my parents did the same for me without ever rubbing it in. I felt gratitude.

It has been a great discovery, the best kind of gift—no promotion or publicity. I know I have received it only many years later.

Love and gratitude. But watch out! There is a powerful enemy waiting in ambush. All of us have a dark side, greedy and tough. We will call it ego. The ego believes the universe should contrive to satisfy its desires. If things do not go the way it wishes, it is angry. It sees others as competitors, therefore enemies. It is suspicious and fearful, afraid of not getting what it craves, or losing what it owns.

The ego distorts and falsifies reality in its favor. It is too frightened to enjoy life. It prevents us from loving and from perceiving beauty. It is captive of fleeing time. It fears death, and so does not really live.

We are free only when, for brief moments, we are able to escape the prison of the ego. There are hard ways and softer ways to do this. Listening to a piece of music or watching the starry sky may be experiences that can absorb us so much, we forget ourselves for a few moments and enter a state of happiness and harmony. That is the soft way. An example of the hard way is being close to death, led into a state of clarity and spiritual strength.

A child can make us forget ourselves in both ways. The soft way is obvious. Children, especially the very little ones, are an extraordinary source of joy, at least as long as they are in a good mood. How can anyone remain greedy, worried, cranky, in the presence of a smiling baby?

Children also show us the hard way. They make fun of our ego, crumble it to pieces, challenge it. We are no longer at the center of our worries. The relationship with a child shows up all our weaknesses which the ego usually so cleverly conceals.

If, instead, our ego wishes to use our children for

self-congratulation, it finds trouble. I remember Vivien's astonishment when she came home from her first nursing mother's groups. She had had Emilio for only a few months and loved hearing how beautiful he was. We thought (and still think) he was special, simply because we had brought him into the world. That day, however, during the meeting, in other people's eyes Emilio was just another baby. There were too many babies for anyone to bother saying hers was special. Since then many similar events have opened our eyes. Seeing that our child is just like others helps us see that we are just like everyone else.

The ego has fetishes: objects, beliefs, or habits to which we give exaggerated attention or importance, and which we think will bring us happiness. Anything can be a fetish—money, sex, objects, ideas, career. Fetishes are the totems of the ego, its most concrete or tangible manifestations. Since they continually distract us from what is most important, fetishes are the most explicit obstacle to love and to a clear, affectionate relationship with others.

Machines are one of my fetishes. In certain moments I find machines, at least certain high-quality machines, irresistibly beautiful—the perfect mechanism, the solidity, the button you press that makes a barely audible click, the circuits and lights, all give me an exquisite aesthetic pleasure.

One day I order a German appliance for milling grain into flour. Freshly ground flour has greater nutritional value. Knowing that the quality of nourishment declines in industrial societies because the freshness and wholesomeness of its products deteriorate, I want my family to have a better-quality grain. This is the official reason for my purchase. The hidden reason is my fascination with this machine. I want to add it to my collection of gadgets.

The device arrives. After praising its virtues, I start to use it. I pour in the whole grains and wait for the flour. But all that comes out is chopped kernels. The machine doesn't work. I am distraught. I set about fixing it. Meanwhile, Emilio, who has been sitting in on the whole event, tugs at my sleeve, demanding my attention.

I am worried. Why is it not working? They have swindled me. Or is it I who am incapable of making it work? I must find a screwdriver and take it apart. And as soon as you start dismantling a machine, you lose yourself in the intricate mechanism. What is this screw for? Is this nut indispensable? What happens if I turn this handle a little more? Emilio continues tugging at my sleeve. He is fed up. He wants to play. I brush him aside impatiently because I am disappointed and annoyed.

Suddenly I recognize the irony. I bought this machine to serve his health, and instead the machine distracts me from being with him. It is a fetish, stopping us from being together and enjoying ourselves and being free. I drop the whole thing and go off to play with Emilio.

The lesson in this story is that a fetish is something that comes between me and another and prevents me from being there, maybe from loving. It hardens me, blinds me, deafens me, and makes me aggressive, all under the guise of offering help. I see a fetish as a device that limits and downgrades love, transforming it into greed. A fetish is based on the implicit belief that some object or idea or event has the magical powers to solve our problems and give us happiness. Yet this very belief is exactly what stops us from loving fully. I am convinced that our capacity to love is inversely proportional to the number and importance of our fetishes.

Love is the one factor that has helped me most to resolve problems with my kids. It is far more practical than logical reasoning. I have adopted a principle: If I cannot resolve a problem with my children, I ask myself how I can do so in the light of love. How can love help me resolve this situation?

Here is an example. We are going to a restaurant for lunch. At the last minute, when we are all ready, Emilio says, "I want a nectarine." However, I dislike being late at a restaurant. I prefer to arrive before it is crowded, when the service is better and the food is fresher. Besides, we are meeting friends there. I want to be punctual. This nectarine will delay us, but never mind—fruit is good for you, and Vivien and I try not to surround food with emotions and prohibitions. With exasperating slowness, Emilio eats the nectarine. I seethe. When he finishes, he calmly announces, "I want another nectarine." But you won't be hungry for lunch. We will be late. They won't keep our table. Our friends are waiting. Explanations, threats, protests, are useless. Emilio wants his nectarine. I could pick him up forcibly and put him in the car, but he would ruin everyone's lunch.

Meanwhile, the minutes are ticking away. I want my children to eat peacefully and not gobble down their food, but I end up telling Emilio to hurry. I point out to him that we are all waiting while he indulges himself. After the second nectarine, Emilio asks, "Another nectarine, please?" This is too much. I am furious. I yell, "Enough! Now do as I say." Emilio cries and screams. Jonathan starts crying, too. Our lunch looks more and more doubtful and remote. It seems an insoluble situation. If I win, I lose, and if I lose, I lose. If I drag Emilio to the restaurant, I lose. If I give in, I lose, too. It is not right for a child to hold the entire family hostage. I do not like to succumb to bullying. Explanations and threats do not work. The atmosphere is poisoned. I don't know what to do.

Then I remember love—the higher principle to which I can refer. I manage to touch the small ray of warmth I still have left in me. Once again, in the midst of the storm, I feel my love for this child. I see his pride, his struggle, his anger, his strength. I also manage to divest myself of the whole weight I am carrying around: my pride, hurry, concern about not getting the table, anxiety over keeping our friends waiting, fear that Jonathan may keep crying, anger at the effrontery. I say, "Okay, Emilio—have another nectarine. Eat it in peace, and take as long as you need." I manage to communicate the basic fact—that I love him. Many experts on child-raising would be horrified. You do not surrender to a tantrum. The story, however, does not end here: I will be speaking about this incident later with Emilio. Meanwhile, he starts his third nectarine, but after one bite he says, "Let's go." And we go.

The important thing is that in the whirlwind of anxiety, anger, and the wish to overpower, I could find love.

And this is the real victory.

Love has many shapes, but its essence is ever the same. Love of your parents and love of your children, love for your mate, affection for a friend, compassion for the suffering, love of God, and, yes, even self-love, can take innumerable forms and variations—and degradations. They may seem light-years apart from each other, and yet they all have in common a precious substance that is warm and healing.

On the other hand, each love has its own peculiar gift or lesson it can offer us. Friendship, for instance, has the special quality of camaraderie that no other love can give. Care for the needy and the disadvantaged carries a unique, profound revelation. Parental love, also, has its own particular gift: It has to do with a sense of privilege. Privilege for the opportunity to bring into the world and then take care of a human being, the feeling that this soul has been entrusted to me and my partner. It is a tie that will last as long as we live. It is at once a responsibility and a gift.

This particular form of love comes to light especially on two occasions—times of distress and moments of achievement. All children are destined to have a large number of small accidents and pains. When they are cranky they may need to sleep or to eat. When they are fearful, they need reassurance. If they graze their knees or are feverish, if they break a toy or lose a game, they need our care and sympathy. But what is for us a small matter is for them a tragedy. They cry, they despair. We know it will soon be over, but they do not. So we come to console, help, cuddle, solve the problem. That is a time in which we especially feel the warmth of our affection.

Then there are the victories: the first breath, the first

time our baby rolls over, sits up, or eats. The first time she walks, makes a friend, learns to swim, or goes to school. And also the more special achievements and triumphs. I recall the time when Emilio played the violin in front of the whole school. There he stood, on stage, alone, in front of three hundred people, his schoolmates and friends, all the pupils, the teachers, many parents. I was anxious that he would make mistakes and be disappointed. But he was calm and concentrated and played his two pieces beautifully. As he played, I felt a great love for him. It was a love that had nothing to do with pride. It was instead a sense of awe, as when we see a flower bloom—except that a child is much more unpredictable than a flower. He will cry and laugh, scream and sing, he will refuse to practice or he will grumble about a violin lesson or instead passionately rehearse and listen to music as if glued to the stereo. And I, his father, have the privilege—which at times feels like a burden, but still is a privilege—to nurture the plant till the flower opens. That is where love, this love that is peculiar to parenthood, shines.

I have a theory about love. I believe its ultimate essence is the Grail we all seek: the sense of oneness, the warmth and happiness, the peace that comes from perfect contentment. That is what we are all searching for. We may look for it under many guises: as the ecstasy of pleasure, the exhilaration of success, or the joy of beauty. We may unknowingly look for it as the momentary pleasure that money or even a drug or the thrill of danger may give us. Yet we are all looking for that same ultimate fulfillment. Parenting gives few easy thrills, much, much work, worries galore, but also the opportunity of spiritual transformation and the sublime reward of love.

Acknowledgments

I want to say thank you:

First of all to Vivien, my pal in this adventure. It is a double thank-you, for making parenthood possible *and* for translating and editing this book. And to our children, for the thousand gifts they have given me.

To John Aherne and Jamie Raab, for the way they edited the manuscript—never forcing a point or interfering with the content, but evoking from me the best that I could give—the perfect editors.

To all those who have inspired and stimulated me: to my teacher and the founder of Psychosynthesis, Roberto Assagioli; to Laura Huxley, with her idea that children are our ultimate investment; to Maria Montes-

Acknowledgments

sori, Ashley Montagu, John Holt, whose writings have been a guiding light for me.

To Dave Cole, Marcella Maharg and Stuart Miller, for their valuable suggestions and corrections.

Piero Ferrucci